JUST A WALK
IN THE SUN

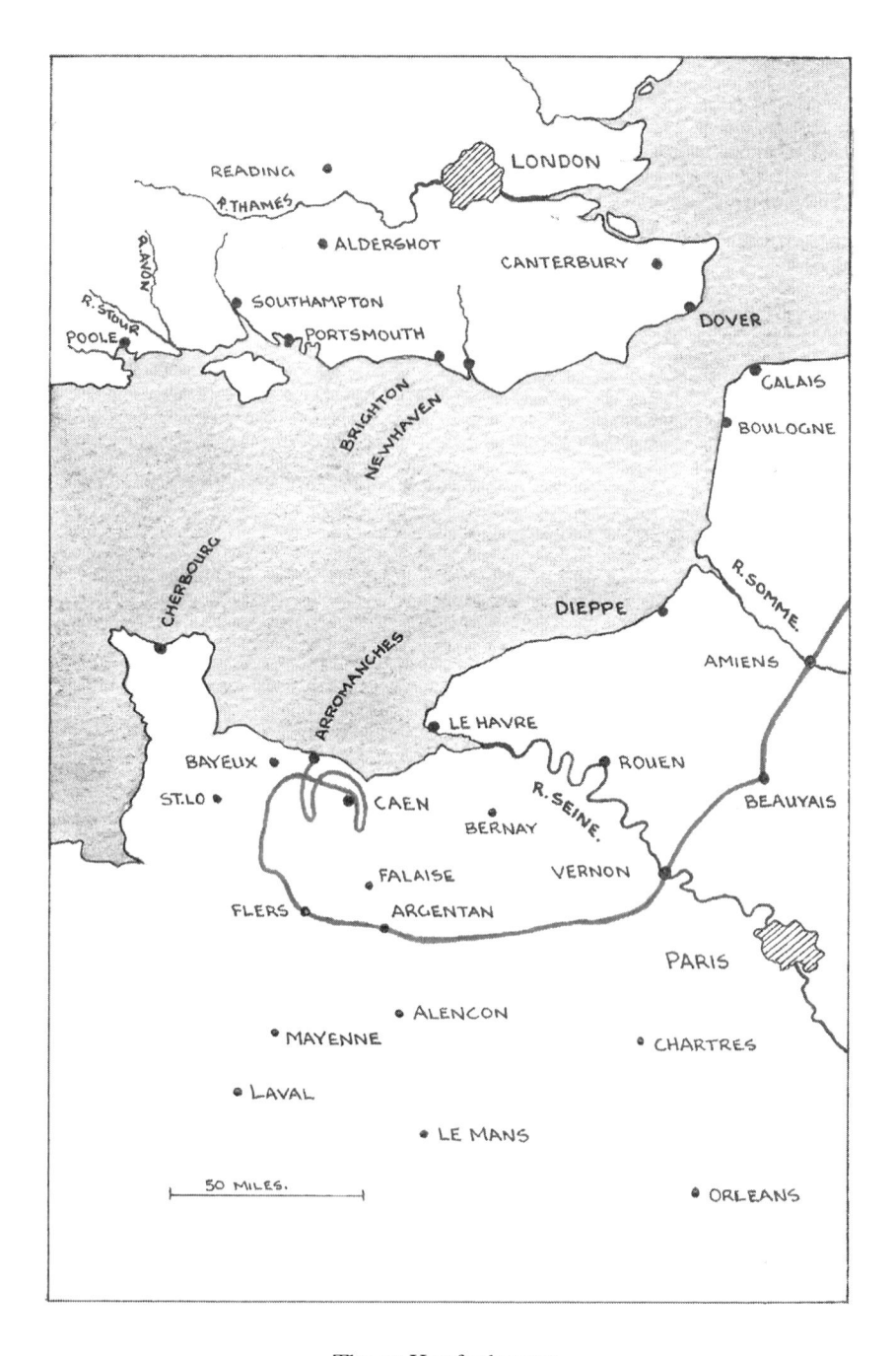

The 1st Herefords route

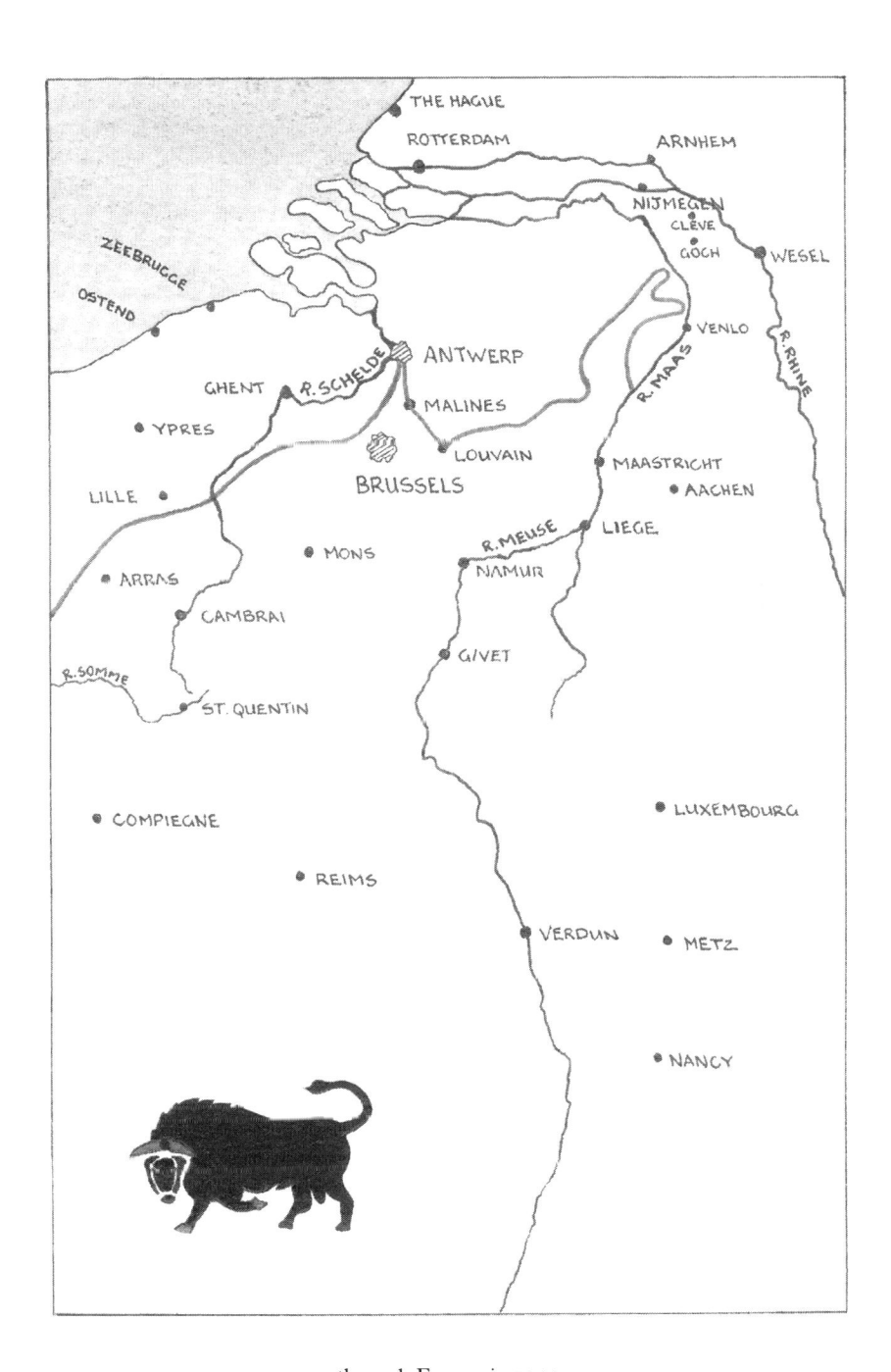

through Europe in 1944

JUST A WALK IN THE SUN

ROBERT STANLEY PRICE

Best Wishes
R S Price
18° July 13.

Published by Nivelo

Copyright © Robert Stanley Price, 2011

The right of Robert Stanley Price to be identified as
the author of this work has been asserted

All rights reserved

Set in Monotype Plantin and Gill Sans by Nivelo
www.nivelo.co.uk

Illustrations, maps and cover art
by Robert Stanley Price

First published October 2002
Second Edition December 2010

Available online from www.justawalk.co.uk

ISBN 978-0-9568767-0-6

THE *prologue*

    9 · *foreword*
  11 · *preface*
  13 · *introduction*

THE *story*

  15 · *the beginning*
  21 · *into battle*
  29 · *the falaise gap*
  33 · *liberation army*
  41 · *one more canal*
  52 · *recovery–rest–reflection*
  57 · *infantryman's war*
  74 · *spring offensive*
  93 · *left out of battle*
  97 · *over the rhine*
106 · *the final assault*
137 · *epilogue*

THE *extras*

141 · *ephemera*
147 · *roll of honour*
154 · *thanks*
155 · *about the author*

FOREWORD

BOB PRICE IS a remarkable man. He would not say he was, but he is. Quietly spoken, self effacing and always keen to underplay his actions, nevertheless Bob is a man worthy of remark. A real Black Country chap, Bob epitomises all the finest qualities of the Black Country working *Mon*. He is loyal to his pals, a dogged fighter, a determined opponent, a generous giver, a modest feller and most of all, a brave bloke who was ready to give his all for his people and his country.

So what makes Bob stand out from all those other Black Country men who share his qualities? Simple, he has written it all down. He has taken up the pen to record his experiences as a foot soldier during the allied invasion of Europe. As Bob points out, many accounts have been written of this massive operation but most are from the perspective of high ranking officers. Important as they are, such accounts do not tell of the experiences, the thoughts and the emotions of the infantry soldier, the one that had to take and hold the ground after all the shelling and bombing.

I have been fortunate enough to meet Bob and to come to know him a little. I interviewed him on my BBC WM show and was deeply affected by his soft words that were as powerful in evoking the horror, fright, tension and excitement of war as any that may have been spoken more loudly. Having read *Just A Walk In The Sun* I find myself as impressed with the power of Bob's writing. Not for him hyperbole or boastfulness, but rather almost a matter-of-fact style that is more successful in bringing across to the reader the events of 1944 and 1945; and Bob's feelings.

Bob's title is a tribute to one of his platoon sergeants. Each morning someone would always ask, 'What are we doing today, Sarge?' often he would reply, 'Oh, just a walk in the sun.' Sadly that sergeant was killed, but his memory will live on through Bob's words and so too will the memories of all those other foot soldiers who slogged and stomped, battled and fought across France and into Germany. Read Bob's book and know why we must remember, why we must never forget. We shall remember.

DR CARL CHINN MBE

PREFACE

JANUARY 21ST 2000 was my 75th Birthday. The events I am about to describe took place over fifty-five years ago and only accounted for one year of my life. Nevertheless it was the most exciting, the most frightening and the most traumatic twelve months of my life. The physical scars healed a long time ago, but the mental scars will always be with me. For many years I was unable to talk about my active service. After all these years I still found some events very emotional and difficult to put into words.

I'd like my story to be seen as a tribute to all my comrades that never came home, I was one of the lucky ones.

Many accounts have been written about the Allied invasion of Europe in 1944, usually by high-ranking officers. I want to tell the other side of the story, what it was like for the private soldier, the one at the sharp end. After all the bombing and shelling he was the one that had to take and hold the ground. The infantry soldier!

The title of this book is in memory of – and a tribute to – one of our platoon sergeants. Each morning someone would always ask,

'What are we doing today, Sarge?'

Sometimes he would reply,

'Oh, just a walk in the sun.'

He was killed in action on 1st April 1945.

INTRODUCTION

A BRIEF HISTORY OF MY ARMY SERVICE

MY ARMY CAREER began on the 4th March 1943. It can easily be divided into three separate parts; the first part you could say was the training period that lasted sixteen months. My primary and corps training was at Norton Barracks, Worcester. I was then posted to the 10th Battalion of the Worcestershire Regiment in Chalfont St Giles, Buckinghamshire. Before the winter set in we moved to New Romney, Kent, on the south coast. Then finally we moved along the coast to Dover. It was there that the battalion broke up and the second part of my service began.

That lasted just ten months, from July 1944 until May 1945. I left England around the middle of July 1944 for France where I joined the 1st battalion of the Herefordshire Regiment in the 11th Armoured Division. It was with this regiment that I did all my active service. Those ten months changed my life forever; I would never be the same person again.

The final part and probably the most frustrating for me lasted the longest, over two years, from May 1945 until June 1947. I served this time with the army of occupation. The fighting ended for me on the 3rd May 1945 in the town of Bad Segeberg near Lubeck. The district is called Schleswig Holstein and stretches from Hamburg to the Danish border. This was the area that the 11th Armoured Division occupied and controlled. The 1st Herefords were stationed at Flensburg, not far from the Danish border in a large barracks on a hill overlooking the town. We stayed there until the following spring of 1946, before moving to Krefeld in the Ruhr. It was while we were there that the battalion was disbanded and I joined the 1st battalion of the Sherwood Foresters in the 7th Armoured Division (Desert Rats) at Delmenhorst, a small town near Bremen. We spent the winter of 1946-47 there, before finally moving to a large barracks on the outskirts of Hamburg, but not before spending a few weeks in hospital with glandular fever. I joined the battalion at Hamburg after leaving hospital at the end of March 1947. My time in the army was coming to a close. Even so, right up to the last few weeks I was doing intensive training on the Baltic coast. I said goodbye to my few remaining mates in June and started my journey home. I was demobbed at York and arrived home on the 30th June 1947.

THE BEGINNING

D-DAY, 6TH JUNE 1944.

I stood high on the cliffs looking out to sea. The weather was unsettled, the sea looked angry with a large swell. I'd never seen so many ships passing through the straits before.

Through my binoculars you could just make out the coast of France and also get a better view of the convoy – ships of all sizes. Down the centre were the large troop carriers and supply ships with their escorts on either side. The swell was so great that even the largest ship disappeared from view as it dropped into the trough between the waves: I found myself anxiously waiting for it to reappear, it seemed ages before it came into view again. I began to wonder why the German coastal batteries hadn't opened fire on such prime targets.

I didn't have to wait long for the answer.

Although I couldn't hear anything, I saw the familiar waterspouts rising around the largest ship in the convoy. I put the binoculars to my eyes and scanned the French coastline where I saw flashes from the guns, something I'd seen many times before. On seeing those flashes the sirens usually sounded to warn the people of Dover to take cover, but today their target was much closer.

I was stationed in the Duke of York's Royal Military School high up on he cliffs above Dover. I'd spent the last three months working on the front and in the harbour building dummy tank landing craft. In fact I became a sailor for a short time, but that's another story! I knew what it was like to be on the receiving end of those one-tonne shells.

I think my worst experience was out on the harbour in a rowing boat, half a mile from shore when they decided to shell. I just sat there terrified while shells exploded all around. Great columns of water, flames and smoke rising fifty feet in the air. The noise was deafening. I just put my hands over my ears and prayed. They were either answered or it was my lucky day, I eventually made it to the shore unharmed.

As the German gunners continued to pound the convoy it was inevitable that they would eventually hit something. A shell finally hit one of the larger vessels, the only casualty I saw. Much to my surprise the vessel continued on its way trailing a little smoke. For a time I thought it was going to be alright, but about half an hour later it began to falter. It slowed right down and began to list. Although it drifted slowly down the channel for many hours and went out of view, it finally sank. That evening I watched many of the survivors coming ashore from the stricken ship, for many of them their war was over. D-day was coming to a close and although I'd only been a spectator my thoughts were with all those men that had landed on the Normandy beaches that morning while I was in my bed fast asleep.

The next morning the atmosphere around camp had changed, the lads were smiling and talking excitedly in groups. They seemed relieved that D-day had finally come, but apprehensive about the outcome. In those days – no television, and very few personal wireless sets – it was very difficult to get any news. The first BBC news bulletin I heard yesterday just said:

> 'In the early hours of this morning, allied troops landed on the coast of France.'

We had to wait some time before we heard any real details about the success of the landings. After a few weeks though, the bridgehead had been enlarged, the Americans were doing well and we hadn't been pushed back into the sea. The weather had also improved!

For us, life went on. Long hours working in Dover harbour continued, the fifty two dummy tank landing craft were now all moored to buoys in the harbour – much the same at Folkestone and other places around the coast. You may think that our job was now finished, but another part was about to begin.

Each morning at first light we had to row out and drop two men on each boat. They were known as the 'simulation of life' parties. Their job was to keep a continuous flow of smoke up through the funnel at the rear of the craft, which they did by burning oily rags in a drum. They also put a line of washing out to give the impression that the crew were on board. The other party were known as the 'rowing party', their job was to row between the boats and shore bringing food, drink and any material required for repairs. Sometimes the canvas panels got damaged and had to be replaced. On good days it was great fun, but when the weather turned bad it was a different story. On one such day we got stranded on one of the dummy craft. As the sea got rougher no one could get to us, I'd never seen it so bad inside the harbour before. The tubular frame began to buckle and some of the canvas ripped and began flapping in the gale force wind. We started to get very worried now, we'd been on the boat for twelve hours and it was beginning to get dark. Imagine our relief when an RAF rescue launch appeared out of the gloom and took us off. We were cold, wet, physically exhausted and very relieved. After a change of clothing, a warm meal and a good nights sleep we were back on the job at first light the next morning. Looking from the shore the next day there wasn't any visual damage. Everything looked very realistic: the washing back on the lines blowing in the wind, wisps of smoke rising from the funnels and little boats moving about amongst them. I've often wondered since, if all the time and energy we put in achieved what was intended.

It's well documented that Hitler and many in the German high command didn't think that the Normandy landings were where the main invasion would come from. For many weeks they still expected the main assault to be in the Calais area, which is why two German army groups were kept there to repel any such assault, while their comrades to the south were in desperate need of support. So perhaps our dummy landing craft did achieve something after all, it would be nice to think so.

By the first week in July it was becoming obvious that the battalion was being broken up and used to replace Normandy casualties. Many had already gone out of the rifle companies so it was only a matter of time before they started on S Company, which consisted of the carrier, mortar, and anti-tank platoons. I was a gunner in the anti-tank platoon and sure enough, one day we heard they wanted seven men from each platoon. There were six guns in the platoon and a seven man crew – including the driver – to each gun. So someone came up with the brilliant idea that the six gun commanders should toss a coin and the losing crew go on the draft.

No prizes for guessing who lost.

The next day we said good-bye to the rest of the platoon and with about two hundred others out of the battalion travelled by train from Dover to

Aldershot. I shall always have fond memories of Dover, it was where I came under fire for the first time, where I stood in the AA gun pits on the front and watched them shooting at the VI flying bombs heading for London, where I used to have lovely Dover Sole suppers at a little cafe standing near the bombed-out promenade.

Good times, good mates.

I never saw any of them again.

The camp at Aldershot was a few miles from the town in open countryside. Everyone was under canvas, mainly bell tents. The administration tent was a small marquee and was also the canteen and dining hall. All the tents were set around a square central parade ground where we fell in each morning for roll call. Although I was only there a few days it was quite eventful.

The second morning we fell in I was picked for guard duty, it was a disaster! We were bundled into a truck and taken to a hill a few miles away. On the hill was a barbed wire stockade, comprising of a tall fence with coils of barbed wire on both sides. Inside were rows of bell tents and a marquee. By now everyone was wondering who the prisoners were and what we'd got to do. We didn't have to wait long for the answer. Outside the gate to the stockade was a bell tent that was the guardroom. The sergeant lined us up – there were thirty-six of us and a corporal. He read our orders out and finally told us what we were dying to know.

'Inside the stockade are over on hundred prisoners from the three services all awaiting trial for murder or armed robbery, so keep your eyes open, especially when it gets dark, is that clear?' he shouted.

Twelve of us were then dropped off in turn around the outside of the stockade relieving the old guard to go back to camp in the truck that brought us. The rest of us just settled down in the heather till it was our turn on duty, which was two hours on and four hours off over a twenty-four hour period. We were lucky with the weather, a nice warm sunny day and at night we lay in the heather looking up at the stars. Just before we were about to be relieved by the new guard, they'd lined up the prisoners inside the stockade for the morning roll call – something they did every morning and evening. We didn't know anything was wrong until the new guard arrived, then panic stations. Thirteen prisoners had dug under the wire and escaped, and on my beat! We were all taken back to camp and the sergeant was arrested.

Back at camp we got cleaned up, had something to eat and were told to stay put. By lunchtime an inquiry was set up in one of the marquees and we were called. By this time I was beginning to get worried, not so much about my position in this mess but because I'd got a twenty-four hour pass which expired at midnight the next day. I hadn't been home since the beginning of March and then only on a weekend pass, so I knew this was my only chance of seeing my family before sailing for France. The inquiry dragged on for most of the afternoon but luckily I wasn't called to give evidence. I was tired, hungry and getting very frustrated when suddenly they said we could go! What a relief, I grabbed my rifle and kit and headed for Aldershot railway station as fast as I could.

I can't remember very much about the journey home except that it took a lot longer than I thought. There were a few other lads heading for Birmingham so we all travelled together. There weren't many trains running and we had to change at least once, that meant long waits in between. We finally reached Birmingham about one o'clock in the morning. There wasn't any transport available for the last part of my journey, my only option was to walk the last twelve miles home. One of the lads was travelling my way so I had some very welcome company, we were both very tired. I'd had very little sleep on guard, and it looked like another night without any. I wished my companion good luck as we parted and did the last part of my journey on my own. It was a warm night and as I turned into our street the sun came up over the trees behind my home. I shall never forget how I felt at that moment, home at last.

The house was all quiet, everyone was fast asleep, and I had to wake them up. They didn't know I was coming so you can imagine the surprise and delight on my mother's face when she opened the door. Just to see the look in her eyes was worth all the frustration of the last twenty-four hours. Next my Dad appeared at the foot of the stairs wondering what all the noise was about. My father wasn't a very emotional person, but today he put his arms around my shoulders and gave me a hug and there was a tear in his eye. When we all settled down Mom cooked me a breakfast, I was starved! Then I jumped on my old bike and raced to my girlfriend's house. Margaret caught the bus to Wolverhampton every morning about 7:30 AM, so I had to catch her before she left home. She didn't know I was coming either so once again another very emotional embrace. Just for a second time stood still, I'd been waiting for that very moment for five months. Shortly afterwards we slowly walked arm in arm the three miles back home completely oblivious to every thing around us. On normal leave you soon begin to count the days, today I found myself counting the minutes. There was such a lot I wanted to say, but couldn't, we were content just to be close. It was soon time for us to catch the bus and return over the same ground I'd walked over just twelve hours earlier.

We reached New Street station in good time, the platform was quite full with servicemen and their families. It's impossible to describe how I felt at that moment: I was about to leave the three most important people in my life. My Mom and Dad and the girl I wanted to spend the rest of my life with.

It was very difficult, but it was important to hide my emotions for the sake of the others, even though inside I was being torn apart. I knew there was only a fifty-fifty chance of them ever seeing me again. The train finally arrived, I hurriedly jumped aboard and quickly found an open window so that we could still talk. It wasn't very long before the train began to move along the platform. We said out last goodbye and within minutes their faces disappeared in the crowd. At that moment I felt very alone, even though the compartment was full with most of the lads I'd travelled up with the day before. If anything helped me it was that everyone in that compartment was in the same boat. Some were coping with it better than others and everyone was in a much quieter mood than yesterday. I think the realisation that we would soon be in France and the consequences of that were sobering thoughts. After another long journey we finally arrived back in camp at Aldershot completely shattered. I didn't need rocking to sleep that night! The next day we got kitted out and after our midday meal we were all loaded into lorries to start our journey to the embarkation port at Newhaven.

INTO BATTLE

WE ARRIVED IN the early evening and quickly started to embark. I don't know what I was expecting but the boats seemed a lot smaller than I thought they'd be. I don't know how many there were but they took around one hundred men per boat. We were packed in below deck like sardines, the whole floor space was covered with double bunks, with just a small clear area at the bottom of the stairway. I remember thinking that if we hit a mine we wouldn't stand a chance. As the last minutes of daylight faded we slipped silently out of the shelter of the harbour into the choppy English Channel. The laughter and joking stopped and everyone settled down on their bunks and tried to get some rest. Sleeping was difficult on a boat that was pitching and rolling and it wasn't long before some were sick. Luckily I wasn't.

I think my experiences in Dover harbour helped a lot that night. I wanted to go to the toilet in the night, which was an experience in itself. First it meant finding the stairs in the dark and going up on deck, the toilet was behind a canvas curtain at the back of the wheelhouse – I say toilet, it was just a large bucket with a toilet seat on top. The trouble was getting there in the dark on a rolling boat with only a single wire safety-rail and a wet, slippy deck. One false move and that would be it, no one would know I'd gone: a sobering thought!

It was a dark, cloudy night and I could just make out the ghostly shapes of the other boats on either side of us. Not a light to be seen anywhere, everything seemed unreal. Only two days ago I was at home with my family and now I was about to embark on the greatest adventure of my life.

I woke to find we'd reached our destination, Arromanches on the coast of Normandy. We were inside the Mulberry Harbour moored to a large floating platform from which ran a pontoon bridge to the shore. We emerged from the hold unwashed, unshaven and bleary eyed – not a pretty sight – and to make matters worse it was raining. On reaching the deck I looked over the side and amongst the debris a dead sailor floated by. I felt sick! We set off in single file along the bridge and it wasn't long before we reached the shore. I shall always remember the day – Friday 21st July 1944.

We continued our journey up the hill through the mud and devastation of the little town until we reached a small camp about five miles inland. We spent our first night in France, rather wet, in an orchard under canvas.

The next morning we awoke to the sun. After a wash, shave and a good breakfast we were ready to move on. Luckily we didn't have to walk too far before reaching our destination, a large transit camp. We were allotted one of the tents, the old anti-tank crew stuck together. By the next morning we were still a bit apprehensive as to what was going to happen next, but we soon found out.

After breakfast we all had to line up in single file, the officer in charge walked along the line and counted off the first fifty. Number, rank and names were taken and in the afternoon they were dispatched in a couple of trucks to join a regiment. The next morning after breakfast saw the same procedure as yesterday, the camp sergeant walked along the row of tents calling us all out on parade. I was just about to leave when my old gun commander Corporal 'Dolly' Doughton whispered,

'Follow me.'

He crawled under the flap at the back of the tent, through a hole in the hedgerow and into a cornfield. We sat there quietly until the parade was over, then returned to our tent. Unfortunately two of our lads were picked in the line up. We had a drink with them that night before saying our farewells. The next morning everybody in our tent followed Dolly into the cornfield, and many more did the same. It was obvious that a lot of us were missing when the rest were lined up on parade, though much to our surprise nothing was done about it. Most of those that had turned out left by truck later that night. The next morning we all went to breakfast as usual, but today it was different: we all had to give our number, rank and name before they let us get our breakfasts. Here was I thinking I'd found a foolproof way of keeping out of the war! Now everyone entering the camp was checked-in, no more standing in line. A list went up on the notice board each morning with the names of those who would be leaving that night. Two days later only Dolly and myself were left, the rest of the old gun crew had gone. It was our turn tonight.

About twenty-five of us travelled by truck up to one of the regiments in the line. We didn't know where we were going or what unit we were joining. The truck slowly made it's way up a dirt track finally arriving at a farm where a sentry stopped us and an NCO led us into a field

'Dig in along the hedgerow tonight and get some sleep, I'll sort you out tomorrow morning. Be as quiet as you can.'

My first night in the line wasn't a bit like I'd expected: quiet, peaceful – not a sound. We had to stand-to one hour before dawn and remain alert until first light, apparently that's the most vulnerable time for the enemy to attack. We had been lucky last night, we found a half dug slit-trench, which saved us a lot of hard work. Although it was July it got quite cold in the night and trying to sleep sitting up with your back against the ends of a trench and your legs side-by-side along the bottom isn't the most comfortable way to spend a night with someone. Now it was getting lighter you could make out the trees and hedgerow at the far end of the field, the grass was wet with dew and the mist beginning to lift. All around us whiffs of smoke began rising out of the grass on the still morning air from those first cigarettes. This peaceful scene suddenly came to life, heads popped up out of the ground, people started to move around brewing tea and getting breakfasts. Someone brought us a large jug of tea, I didn't know anything could taste so good!

We found out we were in the 1st battalion of the Herefordshire Regiment in the 11th Armoured Division. I was quite pleased really – after all it was our sister county – and also being an anti-tank gunner I knew a bit about tanks. By the time we'd all had our breakfasts the sergeant who we saw last night called us together.

'I want you to get into four equal groups.'

Of course I went with Dolly, but was surprised when he insisted that I went in one of the other groups.

'Bob, I know nothing about infantry tactics, I'm a gunner, and you'll be better off without me.'

He was ten years my senior, I'd always respected his judgement so I reluctantly shook his hand and wished him luck. He went to D Company, I went to A Company and I never saw him again. He was killed with most of his section on the 15th August 1944, just sixteen days after joining the battalion. Of course I didn't know he'd died at that time, it was many weeks later and then only by a chance meeting with someone from D Company. A Company were about half a mile down the track from battalion HQ. We proceeded rather cautiously, following our guide. On the way we passed a burnt-out truck, on the ground nearby were the blackened bodies of its two occupants. I'd never seen anyone burned to death before, they had been distorted into grotesque shapes by the intense heat. The one nearest was lying on his back with his fleshless arm pointing to the sky like a final salute. When we reached A Company we were divided up amongst three platoons. Our first job was to dig in and get below ground as soon as possible, luckily we'd just about finished our first slit-trench when we came under mortar fire and everyone dived for cover. This was quickly followed by our own 25-pounders whistling overhead, everyone started cheering and shouting, especially when they heard the continuous explosions as the shells reached their target. That's the difference between a shell and a mortar bomb, you don't hear a mortar bomb until it hits the ground and the explosion is quite a shock, especially if it's close.

One incident that happened that afternoon while the mortars were falling was very painful for me, although my two mates thought it was hilarious. It was such a warm day I'd stripped to the waist to do the digging. Inadvertently I'd just caught the edge of a red ants nest, so while I was sitting in the trench, ants started to go down the back of my trousers. I don't need to explain the agony of what happened next – a bite from one red ant is painful enough. I shot out of the trench and jumped out of my trousers (never mind the mortar bombs). Everybody thought it was great fun watching me jumping about with no clothes on trying to brush off those little red devils. You've heard the saying 'ants in your pants', now I know exactly what it means.

The mortar attack didn't last long after our guns returned the fire. At the first opportunity I plugged the hole where the ants were getting in to the trench, then gathered some straw from an old barn to line the bottom. I was determined to have a warmer and more comfortable night tonight, and I did. I had to take my turn on guard though, one hour on and two off, then all awake one hour before dawn as usual. The straw in the bottom of the trench was a great improvement.

After our breakfast we began to get more organised, the platoon sergeant sorted the three sections out and we were put in platoon HQ. I think at this point I ought to introduce you to the two people that I was going to eat, sleep and fight with for the foreseeable future:

Sparks came from Droitwich, nineteen years old, he ought to have been a rugby player. A gentle giant with a soft Worcestershire accent and a dry sense of humour. He carried the platoon's anti-tank weapon, the PIAT (Projector, Infantry, Anti Tank).

Taffy came from Abergavenny, the opposite to Sparks in every way. A miner all his life, over forty years old, five feet four inches tall, red hair and a big red moustache. If he'd been born a dog he'd have been a Jack Russell. His job was number one on the platoon's two-inch mortar. My job was his number two – he carried the weapon and I carried the mortar bombs. I could see now why we had to be fit, we'd all got quite a load to carry. In my case, besides a full pack and two ammunition pouches I'd got my rifle and bayonet, water bottle, one hundred rounds of ammunition, two grenades and two magazines for the Bren gun, plus eighteen mortar bombs.

The next day was another beautiful warm sunny day, I lay on the grass looking up at the American bombers high up in the stratosphere heading for their targets in Germany. You couldn't hear them, it was the vapour trails that gave them away. Not far away the German 88 mm anti-aircraft guns opened up, you could see the shell bursts in the clear blue sky as they exploded amongst the bombers. By now everyone was watching the drama overhead and it wasn't long before one of the bombers was hit. It started to falter and loose height with smoke pouring from two of its engines.

'Bail out! Bail out!' The cry echoed around the field.

Relief, as one parachute after another opened up and the crew escaped from the stricken plane. In the short time they were in our airspace, three were shot down. I wondered how many would make it back that night. Then suddenly – as if in retaliation – our 25-pounders opened up. High above us an Auster artillery spotter plane appeared to direct the 25-pounders fire. It was circling above us when it received a direct hit from one of our shells. I couldn't believe my eyes: one minute it was there, the next it had gone. It was the first time I'd seen our own men killed by friendly fire, but I'm afraid it wasn't the last.

The next morning I had to go on a two-man patrol, something I'd never done before and I wasn't looking forward to it very much. The corporal in charge said we'd got to check there weren't any Germans dug-in around a crossroads somewhere in front of our forward positions. The more I thought about it, the less I liked it. I could see the corporal wasn't very keen either. We got the map out, planned our route and finally set off around 1100 hours. First we'd got to pass through B Company lines to our right, but after fifteen minutes we hadn't seen a soul. We were lost! Quite understandable really as our map wasn't all that detailed and the countryside consisted of small undulating fields and orchards with little tracks leading in all directions. We'd almost given up, when suddenly we heard someone singing. We went through a gap in the hedge, and there sitting on a bank were two of our lads singing away as if they hadn't a care in the world. As we walked towards them I couldn't believe my eyes and when they recognised me the corporal thought we had gone mad.

'Bloody hell!' they both shouted in a broad Black Country accent.

We were all in the same class at school together, and I hadn't seen them since. After all the backslapping, we had finally found B Company. I said goodbye to my old school mates and they pointed us in the right direction for us to continue our patrol.

The countryside was perfect for an ambush as you couldn't see further than a hundred yards in any direction. By now we had come quite a way, the corporal was a nervous wreck, I suggested we stop and consider our options. We sat down under a tree and had another look at the map – it was a hot afternoon and we were both exhausted. While the corporal was looking at the map I spotted some movement behind a bush some distance in front of us.

We kept very still.

Yes, there was definitely someone there.

I slowly moved out to get a better look, while the corporal covered me. Now I could see the grey of a German uniform, he was lying on his side in the grass. I started to move towards him but he looked up and saw me, raised his arm and smiled. We cautiously moved in.

What we found was a wounded German soldier. How long he'd been there I don't know but he was glad to see us, we couldn't stop him talking. He'd got a nasty wound and had lost a lot of blood – let's say he'd never be a father – so we got him on his feet and with our help we finally got him back to our lines. The company commander was quite pleased we'd brought back a prisoner. We were just glad we'd got back in one piece.

The next day we woke to the sound of approaching tanks – our tanks. This was my first contact with one of our tank regiments. I began to realise why we'd been here resting for the last few days, we'd been waiting for our tanks to be re-armed and brought up to strength again. A week before I joined the battalion our tanks had been in a big battle near Caen, they'd sustained heavy casualties losing 115 tanks and many of their crews.

'Get dressed' the cry rang out. That meant leaving the safety of that hole in the ground, putting on your equipment and be prepared to move out.

I heard that call many times in the next few months and it always sent that tingle of fear and excitement down my spine. It wasn't long before the company were on the move, leading were four tanks of the 2nd Fife and Forfar Yeomanry. We didn't know where we were going or what our task was. In the beginning this was a problem, but we soon began to accept that whoever was giving the orders knew and we would eventually be told, anyway I don't think it helped to know too much.

Today they told us we were going to relieve a company of the guards who were holding a hill they'd captured yesterday. We came under mortar fire but pressed on until we reached the ridge, once there we just changed places with the guardsmen who hurriedly retreated back down the track we came up. We settled in and did any alterations necessary to our new trench.

All around us was utter devastation, the trees blasted, the farm buildings shattered and the air foul with the death-stench of cattle and horses. The pungent smell of high explosive lingering on the air, the smoke and dust of battle belied the serenity of the summer sky. Even though my sense of smell was poor I could still taste death all around. About fifty yards away one of our tanks had been knocked out by a German 88 mm gun, all around were the bodies of guardsmen lying where they had fallen yesterday. Their equipment immaculate, their boots polished, even the two inches of white towel showing below the flap of their haversacks.

So this was what a battlefield was really like.

It was impossible to describe my feelings, and the best way to overcome them is not to analyse events too deeply. Everyone was very quiet, all coming to terms with it in their own way.

I'd come to the conclusion that the standard issue entrenching tool was useless and Taffy agreed with me. The ground in Normandy was hard and stony – what we needed was a good pick and shovel. Whoever could get be low ground level the quickest stood the best chance of survival.

I had a brainwave.

'I wonder if there are any tools left on that knocked out tank Taffy?'

The next minute I found myself running towards it, I had to cross the fifty yards of open ground, so I didn't hang about. On the far side of the tank there was a shovel strapped to the toolbox, just what I wanted. I undid the straps, grabbed it and dashed back to the safety of our trench. It was only then that I noticed the 'Elephant' trademark stamped on the shaft that meant the manufacturer was Yardleys, made only half a mile from where I was born. What a coincidence! All we've got to get now is a good pick and our digging-in problems are solved. By early afternoon we were beginning to wonder how long we had got to stop here, not that we were bothered about moving. Other than the odd mortar bomb it had been very quiet. How quickly things can change!

Sitting in the trench we were watching a pair of US Air Force Thunderbolts circling overhead when the leader peeled off and dived straight at us. We took evasive action and couldn't believe our eyes when he released the 500 pound bomb he was carrying. It whistled over our heads and landed fifty yards away in the next field.

'Watch out!' screamed Sparky, as the second plane did the same.

The noise was deafening, the ground shook and debris fell all around us.

'Bloody yanks! They must be blind!' yelled Taffy. We found out later that in the next field was a knocked out German Tiger tank. They were unable to know that I suppose. We were very lucky today, no casualties.

The next morning we were on the move early. With tank support the battalion moved forward onto some high ground and with very little opposition we were soon dug-in along the ridge. The guards armoured division then launched an assault along the valley, our job was just to give flank protection. We had an easy day, it gave us a chance to clean up a bit and get a wash and shave. Taffy also acquired a pick from a knocked out 15 cwt truck, so we were all set up to beat this hard Normandy ground. Taffy – being a miner – could get a hole out quicker than anyone I knew, whether kneeling down or standing up. We were always first below ground once we'd got that pick, then we let the rest of the lads use it. One thing we hadn't thought of was how we were going to carry it. The same with the shovel. We needed both hands free when we were on the move, Taffy to carry the mortar and his rifle, me to carry 18 mortar bombs and my rifle. This is how we solved the problem. When Taff put his pack on I slipped the handle of the pick down behind it and rested the metal blades across the shoulder straps. It worked a treat! The shovel needed a different approach: I found that if I slipped the handle behind the left ammunition pouch and through my belt with the blade of the shovel flat across my chest it was neatly out of the way. It also gave me protection over a vital part of my body from shrapnel or any other flying objects. That's how we carried them across three countries with out any difficulty, on many occasions they were more vital to our survival than our weapons.

THE FALAISE GAP

I THINK NOW would be a good time to pause from the day-to-day events and look at the overall picture. The countryside we have been fighting in over this last week stretches southward from Bayeux, an undiscovered and inviting country, richly wooded and full of sudden and unexpected panoramas. Numerous little rivers and streams irrigate the region, between the thick hedges the roads wind and fall, broken every hundred yards or so by a corner or junction. The farms are small and white while the villages are small and grey. The land flows with cider and calvados.

This *bocage* was never intended to be a battlefield, the whole character of the region is ill suited to the arts of war. The country is difficult for infantry and almost impossible for tanks. Many hundreds of Britons and Americans were to die in the leafy lanes, fields and woods of the bocage.

Nevertheless, it was here that the first undebatable and irreversible victories were won, here that our troops first advanced without the prospect of subsequent withdrawal. In the bocage – decisively and without doubt – Germany lost the war.

The battles over the next two weeks were nothing spectacular, they consisted of a series of thrusts, strong enough to exploit any weak points in the German defences. Each day was a story of steady progress and firm consolidation. It was decided that owing to the nature of the terrain it was necessary for the closest co-operation between tanks and infantry. It was anticipated that many local engagements would take place, and under these conditions reasonable progress could only be assured if the infantry accompanied the tanks, often riding on them. This system also worked well on many later occasions, and was more or less adopted as standard practice for the advance into Germany. Covered by the firepower from the tanks, the infantry were able to move in and finish the job.

It was about this time that the company commander decided he wanted one man from each platoon to report to company HQ each night as platoon runners. Although company HQ had got radio contact with battalion HQ, all orders given to the platoons had to be verbal or by message. This job for our platoon was divided between Taff, Sparky and me; so every third night I found myself at company HQ. I don't think anything caused more trouble between us three than when we had to decide who's turn it was, you could remember who went last night, but the night before that was another story.

Also, with this type of close contact with the enemy every night we sent out listening patrols a few hundred yards in front of our positions. On one of these patrols I had quite a hair-raising experience. It was a dark night and we were proceeding along a hedgerow when we met a German patrol coming towards us. It was a good job we heard them first, we kept very still as they passed by on the other side of the hedge. I think I preferred a night at company HQ any time.

I shall always remember one such night, at the end of a rather mobile day we pulled into an orchard and dug-in. I lost the argument with Taff again and reported to company HQ for the night. It wasn't a busy night, I think I only had one message to take, although I remember it was raining and very dark so I had a job finding the platoon. By the time I got back to HQ I was soaked. I tried to get under the 15 cwt truck but without much success. I teamed up with one of the other runners and we wandered around the field in the dark trying to find some shelter from the rain. We'd just about given up when we found a little wood shed right in the corner of the field. We opened the rickety old door and curled up on the floor. We were soon fast asleep.

I think what woke me was the sun shining through the cracks in the door. For a full minute I couldn't think where I was and there was someone's boots sticking in my back. I sat up and gave my companion a push,

'Can you hear anything?' I said, standing up.

I opened the door.

The field was empty, not a soul anywhere, we were alone.

'What's that smell?'

It was only then that we realised we'd been sleeping in a toilet.

Luckily we'd been laying the 'right' way round but our trousers and boots were covered, at least it wasn't a bad colour match! We cleaned ourselves as best we could using handfuls of wet grass, forgetting for the moment the predicament we were in. We found the gate out of the field into the lane but we still couldn't hear a sound. I said,

'That's the way we came yesterday, we had better start walking the other way.'

We hadn't got a clue what time it was, the sun was shining, the birds were singing, we'd no idea which way to go. After we'd been walking for about two hours we heard a truck coming down the road towards us. When we were sure it was one of ours we stepped out into the road and stopped it. Were we glad to see someone at last! After a short conversation with the driver he pointed us in the right direction and shortly afterwards we caught up with our column. We walked up the line of vehicles and there sitting on a gate were Taff and Sparky, he was still carrying my breakfast in his mess tins.

'Where the bloody hell have you been?' he shouted, 'You smell like a shit house!'

I thought, if only you knew Taff!

On the evening of the 16th August, armoured cars of the Inns of Court Regiment entered the town of Flers and reported it clear, the next day we entered the town. It was the first town – as opposed to village – we had occupied and for the first time we began to speak of 'liberating' places rather than 'capturing' them. It was also the first time we were greeted by the people – they lined the streets and waved as we walked-by offering us fruit and cider, which was very welcome on such a hot and dusty day. Before this our reception had been very indifferent. It was a great moral booster.

By the time we'd cleared the town and were heading for our next objective everyone was in a happier frame of mind. It was becoming obvious that the enemy was now conducting a planned withdrawal to the east, blowing bridges and planting mines wherever he could. He also left behind organised rearguards if he thought they could hold us up. The lack of opposition in the morning of each day proved this point, it was usually in the afternoon before we overtook his rearguard. This situation was being forced upon him by the increasing threat to his flanks from the north and south. As the pressure increased, his forces in this pocket faced the danger of encirclement south of Falaise.

This is when we first heard the term 'The Falaise Gap', it referred to the only way his forces inside the pocket could escape – the gap between the towns of Falaise in the north and Argentan in the south. With all his transport being forced into this bottleneck it was being mercilessly strafed by the allied air forces and shelled by our artillery until the roads to Bernay were completely choked with smashed and burning transport. Thousands of prisoners were taken and we took our first General. This was the commander of the 276th Infantry Division: Lieutenant-General Kurt Badinski, and with him his staff. That was on the 20th August. Within another few days all the divisions in the pocket were eliminated. With the defeat of his troops in the pocket there was no reason to fight rearguard actions or pursue other such delaying tactics, nor indeed had he sufficient troops left to do so. The only cause open to him now was to retire as quickly as possible behind the next line of defence, the water barrier of the river Seine.

LIBERATION ARMY

With the capture of Argentan by the Americans, a route was cleared through the town. This enabled us to pass through in the night. We were travelling in our three-ton Bedford TCVs (Troop Carrying Vehicles), each truck carried a platoon of infantry – that's about thirty-six men and their equipment. They had three rows of seats running the length of the vehicle with a canvas top. This is how the infantry battalions normally travelled in an armoured division. We covered hundreds of miles this way, although not tonight. The leading troops ran into a few problems, they were delayed by mines, demolitions and blown bridges. We dug-in and spent a peaceful night waiting for the obstacles to be cleared.

On the morning of the 23rd August the whole division was concentrated near the town of Laigle. With the relief of the 3rd Monmouthshire (Mons) Regiment, who were holding the town, the current operational mission of the 11th Armoured Division came to an end.

We settled down for a few days rest before the next phase of the advance. Reinforcement of tanks and men were brought up and we were able to wash and shave and get a change of underclothes. I hadn't had my boots off for three weeks!

We rested, wrote letters and got some sleep. Meanwhile the 43rd Division had made a successful assault across the Seine at Vernon, a Bailey bridge had been put across the river and a bridgehead secured. Now it was our turn!

At 0600 hours on the 28th August the advance began with the 29th Armoured Brigade in the lead with 159th Infantry Brigade, which included the Herefords, following. The first tanks crossed that night, we went over the next day with regiments of the Guards Armoured Division. Ultimately the pursuit was to be carried out with two divisions up, the guards on the right and ourselves on the left. The next few days are difficult to describe, as everything happened so fast. We sat in our TCVs, on the move night and day. What opposition we met was quickly eliminated until we got within thirty miles of Amiens on the river Somme. It was at this point that General Horrocks, our commander, proposed a night march to Amiens. The main object for this bold move was to seize the bridges over the river Somme. Of cause we didn't know anything about this at the time, we thought we were going to stop and hopefully get something to eat and a few hours sleep. Unfortunately we were ordered to press on. The main problem was petrol supplies, the regimental columns had just about enough to get them to Amiens. The leading units were replenished by 2300 hours so we continued on our way. It should have been a moonlit night according to the calendar, but it was a dark night pouring with rain for most of the time. A more serious problem was fatigue; every time the column stopped the drivers fell asleep. It meant someone running up and down the column to wake up the offending drivers and get things moving again.

It must be realised that some of these drivers (especially those carrying petrol) had only had one nights sleep in the last four – whilst we were only going one way, they were travelling both. The nearest supply was fifty miles behind us at the moment, how far tomorrow night was anyone's guess. All petrol was carried in four-and-a-half-gallon jerry cans in three-ton lorries over some of the worst roads imaginable. To move the 11th Armoured Division one mile up the road required one-thousand gallons of petrol. No petrol, no advance!

By 0400 hours we were only a few miles short of Amiens, we disembarked and dug-in on a hill. Taffy was soon busy getting our trench out, it was nice to be doing something again after all the hours we'd spent sitting on those hard seats. The rain had stopped but the wind was cold, we were in the middle of a large ploughed field. I'd acquired a German water bottle which I thought was filled with water but much to my surprise it contained calvados instead. Just what was needed to keep out the cold!

Sparky joined us in the trench and we passed the bottle around, soon we didn't feel the cold at all. By dawn we all felt quite happy. Taffy kept bursting into song, but hymns didn't sound quite right somehow. The sergeant told him to shut up, he could never understand what Taffy said anyway, drunk or sober.

At 0500 hours our leading tanks entered the outskirts of Amiens, within half an hour they were over the first railway bridge and by 0600 hours the centre of the city was reached. For a short time one tank and some infantry put up a stand but were soon eliminated. The operation was crowned with final success when at 1045 hours 23rd Hussars and a company from the 8th Battalion the Rifle Brigade captured intact the main bridge over the Somme. Later another bridge was seized by the 2nd Fife and Forfar Yeomanry. We had been held in reserve for this operation, so by the time we entered the city in the afternoon to take over a section by one of the bridges, the enemy had been all mopped up. We held the city until that evening at 1800 hours, when we were relieved by 151st Brigade of 50th Division, thus releasing us to continue our advance through the night.

Our next main objective was Aubigny, some ten miles northwest of Arras. The German army was now in complete disarray, so much so that at first light each morning we were finding German units travelling in our columns under the misapprehension that they were their own. At dawn one morning divisional HQ found itself alongside an enemy field bakery, accompanied by a Mark IV tank (that was destroyed before it could fire a single shot). Prisoners were becoming a most irritating encumbrance, many hundreds had been captured in the last few days and it was becoming usual at this time to hand them over to the *Marquis* (French resistance) who invariably proved willing to co-operate in this respect. By 1500 hours we had reached our objective for the day and dug-in south of the town of Aubigny. Our leading tanks had made contact with the enemy at 1100 hours this morning on the Arras-Doullens road and notable execution was done.

At the end of the day over a thousand prisoners were captured, including the Chief of Staff of the Somme Corps. During the day numerous flying bomb sites were overrun, they were the first I'd seen, many were reported in the area but off the line of our advance. One certainty: they wouldn't be used again.

Early next morning the relentless pursuit continued, and so – unimpeded except by the delaying actions of the enthusiastic population – the division passed through the battlefields of the first world war. A desolate landscape, pyramids of coalmine waste reaching high above the houses, grey dusty villages and towns, this was the industrial area of France and not pretty place. Nevertheless the enthusiastic welcome the people of the region gave us will never be forgotten by anyone who experienced it.

We were showered with fruit and flowers and if the column stopped we were overwhelmed. On one such occasion I was pulled from the back of our TCV by a Frenchman and his family and taken into their home, which was only a few yards from the road. They had waited over four years for this day and just wanted someone to celebrate this occasion with them. I was poured a glass of wine, the tears of joy running down his cheeks, his wife hugged and kissed me, I felt very humble. I hadn't been in the house many minutes when I heard Taff shouting,

'Bob, we're moving.'

I shook their hands and quickly joined the lads as the column moved off. In each village we went through the welcome was the same. We held our arms out of the side of the truck, so that those along the road could just touch our hands as we went by. The crowds were so dense in places we could hardly get through, the children were so excited I was afraid someone would get hurt, the tank tracks seemed so near their feet.

By early evening we'd reached our objective for the day: Vimy Ridge, a hill rising out of a flat landscape. The whole hill was completely fenced off around the perimeter, that's how it had been since the end of the first world war. We took up our positions on the ridge but found it impossible to dig any sort of trench, the whole hill was covered in brambles and nettles. When we did clear a patch we found there was such a lot of metal in the ground we couldn't penetrate it with a pick or shovel. It was only then that we found out from the platoon sergeant what had happened here some thirty years earlier.

The metal was from the shrapnel of thousands of shells raining down on the ridge, sixty-thousand allied soldiers died there. I don't think many of us had much sleep that night, it was like sleeping in a cemetery, an eerie place. Some of the lads swore they heard moaning in the night, I was just glad when it was time to leave. We found out later why we'd been called upon to spend the night on Vimy Ridge, our brigade commander Brigadier Churcher had fought there all those years ago, well that's the story anyway!

We were told today our next objective was the port of Antwerp some ninety miles away, and ordered to push on there with all speed. The 23rd Hussars led the right-hand column, the 3rd Royal Tank regiment the left. The latter soon met considerable opposition at Seclin and was held up until 1200 hours. The enemy force withdrew after losing seven of his 88 mm guns. Later in the day the 3rd Royal Tank Regiment also had a fight with a small enemy force including a Tiger tank. Sufficient delay had however been imposed, Antwerp was now out of the question for today. The greater part of the division concentrated for the night in the area southeast of Alost. Our first night on Belgium soil, Taffy moaned, picking up the shovel,

'I bet the ground is just as bloody hard as France.'

The best news of the day was the liberation of Brussels by the Guards Armoured Division. Last night our forward tanks had reached the Antwerp highway at Wolverthem, this was to become our main route for the final drive to Antwerp. To reach this highway, first we had to negotiate a route through the town of Boon. I thought we'd seen everything over the last few days, but the enthusiastic welcome from the people of this little town surpassed anything we'd experienced before. When the column stopped they climbed up into the tanks and into the trucks and for a short time everything came to a standstill. I've never been hugged and kissed by so many different women in such a short time before and I don't suppose I ever will again. We found the main bridge at Boon was blown – this was a major problem. At this point however, there appeared a Belgian engineer who offered himself as guide to our tanks. With his expert assistance he took us a route through Willebroeck that led us over the canal there, subsequently we were able to take the eastern bridge over the river Rupel at Boon. Once this was crossed there was nothing in our way until we reached the main bridge outside Antwerp itself. Apparently this was mined, barred by anti-tank obstacles and covered by machine gun fire. Under cover of a smoke screen, 3rd Royal Tanks and a company of the 8th Rifle Brigade attacked and soon cleared the defences, what other opposition there was soon evaporated. By the time we got there it was all over, 159th Brigade was then given orders for further clearing up operations. They estimated that the German garrison was at least five-thousand strong. The section of the city we were given turned out to be clear – the civilians confirmed this. At this point I can vividly remember I was bursting for a pee! In the country, no problem, but walking down a street full of people and shops, that's a bit different. I was getting desperate when we suddenly came across a toilet: it was just a tiled recess between two shops. I didn't waste any time, I was up on the step like a shot. What happened next was a complete shock. Across the road was a cake shop, two girls out of the shop dashed over and grabbed me, then with a large pair of scissors cut the divisional signs off the sleeves of my battledress blouse. I couldn't stop what I was doing and you don't argue with anyone with a large pair of scissors in that position! They only laughed at me afterwards through the shop window, knowing full well I couldn't do anything about it.

We'd had a fairly easy day, but less than half a mile away it was a different story. At 1600 hours 4th Kings Shropshire Light Infantry (KSLI) were given orders to establish themselves in the central park in the town. The battalion reached the edge of the park without incident but found the park was strongly defended with many pillboxes and concrete emplacements. After a fierce battle lasting four hours they overran the German positions and captured the garrison Commander, General Von Stollberg and six-thousand prisoners. For the lack of more suitable accommodation they locked them all up in the zoo. This later resulted in the commanding officer receiving a letter from the war office saying that Germany had complained through Geneva of the gross indignities inflicted on the German army by the 4th KSLI in Antwerp.

Our tanks reached the dock, 3rd Mons were ordered to secure the sluice gates, upon which the preservation of the port depended. A thorough examination of the whole dock area was made, this revealed that the port itself was virtually undamaged. Back at divisional HQ I expect they would say we'd had a successful day, but we must always remember the lads that died to achieve this success. Thirty infantrymen were killed in Antwerp and probably more than sixty were wounded. Our job done, we returned to the outskirts of the city and dug-in alongside the main road to Brussels. We sat down on the side of the trench and had a smoke, it would be dark soon and we were eagerly waiting for the evening meal to arrive. On the other side of the road an anti-aircraft gun had been set up in the garden of a house, the crew of four were working on the gun. As we sat there quietly enjoying our cigarettes a most unusual drama began to take place. It sounded like the women from the house were arguing with the gun commander, but really she was just excited after the events of the day and wanted to show her gratitude in any way she could. What happened next came as a shock, especially to the gun commander. She went into the house and brought out her four daughters. All work on the gun stopped as the women deliberately handed over one of her daughters to each member of the gun crew. Taffy looked at me in amazement,

'Just our luck to be dug-in on the wrong side of the bloody road!'

Sparky winked his eye at me and turned to Taff,

'If we'd have been over the road you wouldn't have been much use, you're too old Taff, they want young virile blokes like me!'

Taffy blew his top! He could never see that Sparky was winding him up, everyday he fell for it. Luckily the meal arrived, otherwise it might have ended in a fight.

Quite early the next morning, the locals started to gather around our dugouts – mainly children and teenagers. They were curious to see close-to what a British soldier looked like, most of the younger ones had only seen German soldiers. Then someone wanted our autographs – that started something. In no time queues began forming at each trench; Taffy soon got everyone organised. I must have signed my name hundreds of times that morning. I remember one little old lady handing me a book to sign, she was very smartly dressed and spoke perfect English,

'How does it feel, behaving like a film star?' she asked.

'Alright,' I replied, 'but the money isn't as good!'

She laughed.

We were interrupted by the platoon sergeant coming towards us.

'Get dressed lads, we're moving out.'

Our task for the day was patrolling the dock area, so we said our farewells to the little crowd that had gathered and set out for the docks. That night we slept in an empty house on a bare wood floor, not very comfortable. It was the first time I'd slept in a house since leaving Dover in July.

Before moving on I think a few facts might be of interest. In the six days since the division had crossed the Seine it had covered 340 miles, and on five of those six days we had been obliged to fight. All the way from Caumont in the *bocage* – some 580 miles – and for that matter all the way from the beaches, the tanks had travelled on their own tracks. Never once had they been lifted by transporters. By the time they reached Antwerp many of the tanks and self-propelled guns had done considerably more than the mileage prescribed for them. A few fell by the wayside, but on the whole the Shermans had stood up very well to this severe test of their mechanical reliability. The strain imposed on the tank crews over long hours of noisy confinement in hot and dusty conditions should not be forgotten either.

It was about this time in the campaign that the way we were fed changed. Until now we had lived on 'fourteen-man packs', which meant a wooden box containing twenty-four hours of rations for fourteen men. It contained mainly tinned food such as corned beef, steak and kidney, sponge pudding, tins of fruit, tea, sugar and hard biscuits. There was also a small bar of plain chocolate and seven cigarettes (each). The problem was no facilities for cooking anything so it meant opening a tin and eating it cold. We were so hungry we could eat almost anything, and did. Just imagine eating half a tin of corned-beef and changing with someone else – someone who was halfway through a tin of treacle pudding or perhaps sardines. I hadn't had a proper cooked meal since joining the regiment and no bread or potatoes at all! Now with more hours of darkness the company started cooking a proper meal and bringing it up to us after dark. Of course there were times when they couldn't reach us and we had to go without, then we had to eat anything we could scrounge. Shortage of cigarettes was a bigger problem.

There's no doubt that this was a much better system and as the weather got colder it was the one thing that we looked forward to at night, that hot meal, even if sometimes you had to have your pudding in the same mess-tin. We also started to get a hot breakfast – mainly porridge, sausages or bacon – a much better way to start the day than before!

Merxem was a suburb of Antwerp that lay on the northern bank of the Albert Canal. On the 6th September the 4th KSLI were ordered to make an assault over the canal and establish a bridgehead so that the engineers could construct a bridge the following night. At first light the attack went in and they established a small bridgehead against fierce opposition. But in the middle of the morning the enemy counter-attacked with three infantry companies and five tanks, isolating the KSLI in a factory. The presence of the tanks at this early stage was unfortunate, the only anti-tank weapons they had was the PIAT, which soon ran out of ammunition. Enemy shelling continued on an increasing scale throughout the day and with the factory surrounded it was impossible to get supplies over to them. An attempt to reinforce the battalion under cover of darkness proved impossible. Two companies of 3rd Mons and two troops of 23rd Hussars tried to reach them from the southeast corner of the docks. This force was held up by a roadblock – strengthened by mines and covered by heavy fire. The same evening the Germans put in a counter attack on the sluice gates and although this was beaten off by the 3rd Mons the enemy strength in the whole area north of the port was clearly such that no bridges could be constructed under these circumstances. It was finally decided that a further determined effort to advance north would be altogether too costly a venture. At 1530 hours under cover of intense artillery fire, 4th KSLI were bought back across the canal in assault boats, not a single casualty being incurred during the evacuation.

ONE MORE CANAL

As the original plan of pushing northward into Holland over the Albert canal had ended in failure, we awaited our new orders. These we received late on the 8th September, so at 0900 hours on the 9th, the move began: not north, but east via Malines and Louvain, and by nightfall the division was concentrated south of the canal near Beeringen. That evening we crossed the canal by a new bridge constructed alongside the Guards bridge at Beeringen. Then near the village of Helchteren we met our new partners the 2nd Fife and Forfar Yeomanry. Over the next few days we had reasonable success against considerable opposition, taking five-hundred prisoners in one day. With the virtual clearance of all enemy formations from the area between the Albert and Mesue-Escaut canals north of the US sector we had a very welcome short period of rest.

Taffy dug our trench in a derelict garden, while I took the mess-tins to go for our evening meal. The company cooks had set up in an old barn about a quarter of a mile away, so it was quite some time before I got back. By now it was dark and I couldn't find the trench or Taffy. When I said derelict garden, that's exactly what it was, brambles, overgrown roses, grass waist high. With both hands full I staggered up and down the garden calling,

'Taffy?'

But not a sound.

I eventually found the trench alright: I fell in it, right on top of Taff who'd fallen asleep in the bottom! The mugs of tea went one way, the mess-tins the other. Taffy let out a blood-curdling scream that brought half the platoon crashing through the bushes. Someone struck a match.

Taff's face was covered with blood where the studs in my boot had ripped a gash down his forehead. We put a bandage round his head and salvaged what was left of the meal. I wasn't his favourite person that night. By first light the damage to his face didn't look too bad, Sparky said it was an improvement. That day the three platoons closed in around company HQ in a more defensive position, and that's how we stayed for the next six days. I was always very thankful for that rest, particularly as the next day I became ill with sickness and diarrhoea, as were a lot of the other lads. The battalion MO gave us some tablets, which helped, and the weather was dry, which was another bonus. I remember digging a hole and sitting by it night and day, too frightened to move for three days. By the end of the week we were better, but very weak, when the sergeant said,

'Get dressed.'

That's the exactly what we had to do, although I don't know how I got through the next few days! I remember it was at this time we crossed the border into Holland and the opposition was getting tougher. No sooner had we got across one canal than we came face to face with another. It must be remembered that these waterways were much larger than in England, and with all the bridges destroyed over them each one required a plan to be made to overcome the problem, the deployment of the unit to make the assault, the engineers to build the bridge, and finally the armour to pass over as quickly as possible to support the infantry, this unglamorous job the Royal Engineers did throughout the campaign always amazed me. Whatever the problem they seemed to overcome it in the shortest possible time, and invariably in the dark. Their value to our success especially in Holland would be impossible to assess. By the 21st September I was feeling fit again and eating anything I could lay my hands on, and Taff's head had healed alright where I had trodden on him. I knew he was alright, he was moaning about everything again.

All along our front we'd made steady progress since we'd had our weeks rest, today we were clearing the town of Zomeren, it was hard going. By that evening sixteen of our lads had paid the ultimate price. I knew one of them well; he lived in my own town, a few doors away from where I was born. Sometimes I received our local weekend paper from home; I'd never be able to share it with him again.

Just beyond the town lay our next barrier, the Zuid-Willems Canal. That evening at 2100 hours it was decided to send two companies of the Herefords across the canal to establish a bridgehead so that the engineers could put a bridge across under cover of darkness. A Company was one of the companies chosen to do the job. I remember having to pull our assault boat up a steep bank to reach the canal, and it took about four trips across to get our platoon on the other side. All this was done as quietly as possible in total darkness. The other platoons in the company were doing the same on either side of us. Not a sight or sound of the enemy! We then clambered down the embankment and spread out, one platoon to the left, one to the right and our platoon forward about two-hundred yards.

Company HQ dug-in at the bottom of the canal embankment. Much to our surprise, and relief, still no sign of the enemy. We did have one big problem though – we couldn't dig in! As soon as we started to dig a hole it immediately filled with water, so we had to pile the soil up around us to form a barrier. By now one of our searchlight batteries had switched on. By shining on the clouds above us, it gave the engineers that little extra light for bridge building. We used to call it 'Monty's Moonlight'. In a couple of hours we'd built a formidable line of trenches. We then crouched behind our defences waiting for the inevitable attack. By 0200 hours the tension was beginning to creep in, the lads were getting irritable and restless, this was just the opposite to what they'd expected. Then suddenly the silence was shattered by an exploding mortar bomb a few yards in front of us, followed by another and another, all around us. We flattened ourselves against the ground and waited for the bombardment to stop. The attack was intense for a time, all work had to stop on the bridge until the mortar attack had finished. It stopped as suddenly as it began, we then came under heavy small arms fire from the German infantry as they pressed home their attack from two sides. For the next hour all hell was let loose, tracers ricocheting in all directions all around us. At one stage they over ran company HQ behind us and we had to open fire on our own HQ. Our Bren gunner heard a noise just left of our position and opened fire, there was a scream as the rounds found their target, but he didn't die, he moaned and groaned all night. So much so the Bren gunner tried to silence him several times but it was a long time before he went quiet. What I couldn't understand was why every attack stopped ten yards in front of us, why didn't they over run us? One chap was very persistent, he kept returning to have a dual with our Bren gunner until his machine gun finally jammed, he cursed, but couldn't fix it, finally retreating into the darkness. Eventually all firing stopped, Taff and Sparky were alright and the Bren gunner and his mate in the next position, but we didn't know if we were the only ones left in the platoon. Dawn broke, a proper September morning, very misty and quite cold. What with all our digging and the mortar bomb craters it looked like a first world war battlefield. Company HQ was still covered by mist so we didn't know whether they were still there or not. For the next thirty minutes we waited anxiously for it to get lighter and the mist to rise.

Suddenly Sparky whispered,

'Can you see the smoke?'

Sure enough all over this little battlefield you could see the smoke from dozens of cigarettes rising out of the ground. We all heaved a big sigh of relief; we'd survived another night.

I sat down in the corner of the trench and took the letter from my pocket, it was too dark to read it last night when the mail was delivered and I remember thinking, I hope I'm 'still' here tomorrow to read it! It was from my girlfriend. For a few moments my thoughts were lost in memories of our last day together, it seemed a long time ago now. I read the words of love and hope for our future and a speedy end to this conflict. The letter ended, and in the corner, a lipstick imprint of a kiss. The crunch of a mortar bomb exploding nearby quickly brought me back to reality. As the mist lifted and it became lighter we looked around to see exactly where we were. Much to our surprise a few yards in front of our positions was a water barrier, also down our left hand side, probably a drainage ditch. It was about four yards wide and filled almost to the top with stagnant green water. No wonder they couldn't get to us last night, we couldn't have picked a better defensive position if we'd tried. Then again, if we had walked a few yards further in the dark last night I dread to think what might have happened.

Company HQ were alright, they'd all moved out before the Germans attacked last night. Our combined fire drove them out later in the night; the trenches were empty at first light this morning. Our casualties were light, none in our platoon at all. We only found one dead German, the one our Bren gunner shot, he'd got his trousers down around his ankles, what a time to be took short!

The engineers finished the bridge, then under cover of a heavy barrage from our 25-pounders the tanks of the 2nd Fife and Forfar Yeomanry and the 4th KSLI started crossing over the bridge. They'd no sooner cleared the crossing when they came under fire from German anti-tank guns, the first four tanks were knocked out. The second troop pressed on courageously against heavy fire and with the accompanying infantry soon eliminated all the enemy guns. The nearby town of Asten was quickly occupied in spite of heavy small arms fire and by 0900 hours our foremost tanks were moving towards Ommel.

All this activity was happening over to our right. Our section was quiet, just the odd mortar bomb from time to time. We settled down and tried to get some rest. About 1000 hours I thought I recognised someone who walked across the field behind us, he stopped and talked to one of the lads in seven platoon. To satisfy my curiosity I walked over to them, and sure enough it was a lad who lived in the same street as me. Although he was older and I hadn't seen him for a few years he recognised me right away. It was nice to talk to someone from your own home town again, the people we both knew and what they were doing now. I said cheerio and started to walk back to our trench. I hadn't quite got there when a mortar bomb dropped behind me. I looked back in time to see them both fall to the ground; the bomb had exploded right at their feet. I hit the ground and stayed there for a few minutes, nothing else happened so I jumped up and ran back. They were both dead. I slowly walked back to Taff and Sparky and sat on the side of the trench, I was shaking in complete shock and Taff put his hand on my shoulder,

'That was bloody close.'

A few minutes earlier and it would have been me lying there in the mud. It took me a long time to get over that incident, seeing someone you've known all your life die that way. If there's one thing I learned from this experience, call it luck if you like, but if you're in the wrong place at the wrong time, you're dead, so it wasn't worth worrying about it. Take the usual precautions and keep your head down when you could. At the time I thought I shall have closer calls than that – and I did!

We spent another night at the same place before moving on towards the town of Deurne the next morning. Our troops met fierce opposition up this road yesterday afternoon, the enemy made determined counter attacks, the first two from the south, and the last from the north. These were all beaten off and by dusk 159th Infantry Brigade were well established in their bridgehead. Our main problem tonight wasn't the enemy, it was hunger – we hadn't had anything to eat for two days. Luckily we'd got cigarettes; otherwise there would have been trouble. There was a big cheer and a few choice remarks when the cook's wagon finally arrived that night.

The next few days we made reasonable progress. One of our jobs was to clear the wooded country between Helmond and Deurne. It was about this time that the weather deteriorated, until now it hadn't been too bad, now every day we had rain. Movement became difficult, especially for the tanks.

We found ourselves remaining in the same place for days at a time, it became very muddy everywhere, we just had to wait for a break in the weather. It gave us a chance to build a really elaborate trench with our own dry sleeping quarters lined with straw, the roof built with logs covered with soil and finally finished with a layer of turf. We were having to live in holes in the ground like animals, so why not imitate them! I know it raised a few eyebrows amongst the rest of the platoon when it was finished. Having a miner as a mate was a compensation when it came to digging trenches. With the longer nights we were also able to get a few more hours sleep. Over the last two months we'd been awake twenty hours a day!

With an improvement in the weather it was time for us to be on the move again. We were therefore to hand over our sector to another formation, which rather surprisingly turned out to be the 7th US Armoured Division. On the 30th September they assumed control and prepared for an immediate push towards Venlo. Our part in this operation was limited to giving artillery support and garrisoning the little town of Meijel, this meant watching the Deurne Canal, which ran along the eastern side of the town.

Our company arrived in the afternoon and took over from the American garrison. Our force was much smaller than theirs so we had to close in around the centre of the town at night, otherwise we would have been too widely spread and therefore more vulnerable in the dark. Things didn't start very well for us; we hadn't been there very long when we lost the company commander. He was hit by shrapnel from spasmodic shelling, which continued throughout the day. We dug our trench in the grass verge against a low garden wall at the end of a driveway to a detached house. This gave us a good field of fire up and down the road. The house stood about ten yards from the road and looked undamaged from the front, we used the front downstairs room to sleep in. The rear of the house came as a bit of a shock, it was devastated, all the rear wall and part of the roof had collapsed into a pile of rubble, yet standing there in the middle of this once lovely room was a baby grand piano. It was covered with plaster and debris but otherwise undamaged. We had a good musician in the platoon, his eyes lit up when he saw the piano but the sergeant soon realised what he was thinking,

'Forget it,' he said, 'don't touch that bloody piano.'

By nightfall the sky cleared and the moon came up, it went very quiet. It was our turn on the Bren gun; we sat on the side of the trench with backs against the wall cupping our hands around lighted cigarettes. It was getting quite cold now. This little town was an eerie place, the moonlight cast long dark shadows all around us. It was so quiet, not a sound anywhere. We found ourselves talking in whispers, we'd been told the enemy were inquisitively inclined, and nightly incursions could be expected across the canal.

Suddenly the silence was broken, it made us both jump, but not in the way we'd ever imagined. From behind the house the opening chords of The Warsaw Concerto blasted out from that baby grand piano.

'Jack Carrol!' we both shouted, jumping out of the trench and racing round to the back of the house.

There sitting on the stool was Jack, his hands pounding up and down the keys as if he was on stage performing in front of an audience. The moon shone down on him like a spotlight, it was exactly the same setting as in the film Dangerous Moonlight – where this piece of music came from – except this was Holland, not Warsaw. I don't suppose he was playing much more than a minute, but it certainly stirred things up a bit; the platoon sergeant was furious and immediately put him on 'Open Arrest', the punishment deferred to a later date. Give Jack plenty to do and there wasn't a problem, but he soon got bored with all the hanging about. He was a one off, a maverick; he just couldn't cope with army discipline. In action he was a brilliant soldier, he seemed to thrive on danger, and was always the one out in front. In fact he was awarded the Military Medal (MM) for bravery before the campaign was over.

All the excitement over we went back on guard to finish our two-hour duty, everyone else went back in the house and soon everything was quiet and peaceful again. The next hour seemed to drag, we were both feeling pretty tired by now, when suddenly from out of the house came a loud bang followed by a muffled scream. Then total silence!

'What was that?' Taff whispered.

'Go and have a look.' I replied.

'No way am I going in there on my own, I'll fetch the sergeant.'

I put the Bren gun on the wall pointing towards the house, while Taff went down the road to look for the sergeant. He seemed to be away for ages, then I could see them both returning up the centre of the road in the moonlight. Still not a sound from the house! I stayed with the gun while Taff and the sergeant disappeared into the house. I could see a light through the window as someone struck a match. A few minutes later, Taff came out of the front door and walked towards me, he was laughing quietly to himself.

'Well,' I said, 'what happened?'

'One of the lads went to sleep on top of a wardrobe and fell off,' he replied.

'Anybody hurt?' I inquired

'No but he fell on the table and smashed it to pieces!'

What a night! We didn't get much sleep and I was glad when dawn broke and Sparky brought us a mug of tea, it was quite a cold start to the day.

In our old sector the Americans had started with high hopes of breaking through the strong enemy positions situated amongst the large belts of trees that guard the town of Overloon. After five days of endeavour and heavy casualties, a new plan was revealed. After a week in Meijel, the idea of employing the 11th further north had now been abandoned, instead, we would relieve our old friends the 7th Armoured Division between Deurne and the river, they in turn would hold a section on our right from Deurne to Meijel.

We dug-in alongside a large wood; the weather was terrible with almost continuous rain. The main offensive was postponed until the 12th October because of the rain, then the 3rd Infantry Division passed through our positions to operate towards Overloon and Venray as the Americans had done before. If they were successful we would pass through them and advance on the villages of Horst on the left and Amerika on the right. I always thought this was a very unusual name for a Dutch village, it became quite famous and eluded capture until November; mainly because of the weather, which turned the roads into a quagmire making them impossible for tanks or wheeled vehicles. It was the 1st Herefords that finally occupied the village without opposition on the morning of the 22nd November 1944.

In spite of this terrible weather 159th Brigade were quite active and put in several local attacks against the enemy positions along our left flank, these were highly successful and yielded a number of prisoners. One of them was distinguished by a famous exploit which gained the Victoria Cross for Sergeant G. H. Eardley of the 4th KSLI single-handed, with a Sten gun and a few grenades, this NCO destroyed three successive machine gun posts manned by the redoubtable paratroops, a performance which not merely staggered all who saw it, but also ensured the success of his battalion in its task.

By the 16th October, 29th Brigade had crossed the Deurne Canal and were making steady progress towards Meerselo. In the meantime the American operation to establish a bridgehead over the canal on the Deurne-Venray road had met with stiff resistance, and although a bridge was constructed during the night the division was not in a position to continue the advance. A decision was therefore taken to shift 159th Brigade right round into the Deurne area and move them through the American bridgehead the next morning. So on the morning of the 17th October we found ourselves sitting on our tanks in the middle of Deurne waiting for orders to start our advance up the road to Venray. It was while we were there that I saw my very first jet aircraft, a German Messerschmitt Me 262 *Schwalbe* ('Swallow') fighter. The roar from its engines made us jump, we'd never heard anything like it before, everyone looked up as it streaked across the sky. By 0900 hours we began our advance, I was on the back of the second troop of tanks and with the canal only three miles away it didn't take us long to reach the first American troops dug-in on either side of the road. We moved cautiously up the road towards the bridge – it was a typical Dutch road, raised above the surrounding fields with an avenue of trees on either side. The silence was broken by the first mortar bombs falling, about two hundred yards further up the road. We dismounted and continued our advance on foot. Some of the tanks moved down onto the fields but immediately got bogged down. We then came under a ferocious mortar bomb attack; we took cover in the ditch that ran on either side of the road. In a few minutes it was chaos, I pressed myself into the soft earth as hard as I could. All around there were cries from the wounded as the shrapnel from the bombs found their targets. What happened next is hard to explain, a mortar bomb exploded where my feet should have been, and yet I felt no pain. I then realised I couldn't feel anything from my waist downwards – it was completely numb. I was terrified to look over my shoulder and see if my legs were still there. The first person to reach me was Jack Caroll,

'You've got a Blighty there Bob,' he said 'Are you hit anywhere else?'

I looked back and my feet were lying in the crater from the bomb, I must have had my legs wide apart when the bomb exploded! There was a hole in the front of my left leg just above my ankle and a small piece of shrapnel had gone right through my right foot, also a much larger piece in my right upper arm, I wasn't bleeding anywhere. In five minutes those bombs had killed nine of my mates and wounded thirty-three others, I was one of the lucky ones.

The first lull in the mortar attack the wounded were picked up and taken to the nearest field dressing station, a marquee in a field just behind the lines, there the wounds were dressed. Serious cases were dealt with as soon as possible by a team of army surgeons. When transport was available we were moved further down the line to an old school that had been converted into a field hospital, that's where we spent our first night. By now the numbness in my legs had gone. As each hour passed I could feel myself relaxing as the tension slowly melted away, I felt a great sense of relief. My war was over, if only for a few short weeks. Tuesday the 17th October 1944 is a day I shall never forget.

The next day we were transferred to a hospital in Brussels.

No. CAS/K.
(If replying please quote above No.)

Army Form B. 104—81A.

It has not been reported into what hospital he has been admitted, nor are other particulars known, but in the event of his condition being considered by the Medical Authorities as serious or dangerous this office will be notified by cable and you will be immediately informed. In addition he will have been given every facility for communicating with you himself.

Office,

...er 1944

MADAM,

I regret to have to inform you that a report has been received from the War Office to the effect that (No.) 14552923.

(Rank) Private.

(Name) Robert Stanley PRICE.

(Regiment) The Herefordshire Regiment.

has been wounded, ~~and was admitted to~~ in North West Europe.

on the 17th day of October 1944. The nature of the wound is B. Wound Left Leg.

I am to express to you the sympathy and regret of the Army Council.

Any further information received at this office as to his condition will be at once notified to you.

Yours faithfully,

[signature]

Lieut. Colonel.
Officer in Charge of Records.

IMPORTANT.—Any change of address should be immediately notified to this Office.

War Office telegram sent to Margaret, October 1944.

RECOVERY–REST–REFLECTION

The 108 British General Hospital was a large old hospital, probably built in the late 1890s. There were twenty-seven beds in the ward I was in, all soldiers recovering from wounds. Some were like me with only flesh wounds, others in a more serious condition with limbs missing or shot up pretty badly. The courageous way these men behaved throughout amazed me. They were the most cheerful, the first to see the funny side of any situation and I know at times they were in a lot of pain. It was in this ward that I first encountered the drug penicillin, it was in short supply and was only given to the more seriously wounded, it saved many lives.

On the 22nd October it was my turn to go into the theatre and have the shrapnel removed from my leg and arm. They left the wounds open for a time, which made dressing them a bit unpleasant because they were much larger now and the dressing invariably got stuck to the wound every time it had to be changed. The chap in the next bed had lost his leg, so it doesn't need much imagination to picture the pain he went through everytime they redressed it. I felt ashamed when I shouted out once when my dressing stuck, it was nothing compared with what they had to put up with.

Another experience I shall never forget is being given a blanket bath by a seventeen-year-old Belgium nurse, she bathed everyone in the ward that day. To coin a phrase, she didn't leave any stone unturned. I couldn't see an English nurse doing the same. Talking of English nurses, the night sister on our ward was the most beautiful woman I'd ever seen. I know at nineteen I may have been a little naive, but every man in that ward thought the same. Her father was a regular soldier serving in India, he'd got red hair and a big red moustache and her mother was Indian. What a combination! Her complexion was like someone with a lovely suntan, large green eyes and dark, waist-length hair, which she kept in a bun when she was on duty. She was tall with a figure to match a beautiful smile, but her greatest asset was her compassionate nature. Every night she would spend time at each bedside, reassure her patients that were in pain, hold their hands, give pain killers if required, write letters for those who couldn't because of their injuries. She listened to problems and sorted them out if possible; nothing seemed too much trouble for her. Then one night she didn't turn up! Can you imagine our dismay when we learned she'd gone on days on another ward. The sister that replaced her was alright, but the nights were never quite the same again. I'd been hoping to get a flight back to England from Brussels but the weather had been so bad all the planes had been grounded for a week. On the 31st October I left Brussels and travelled overnight by train arriving late afternoon at the French city of Rouen on the river Seine. There I was admitted to the 6th British General Hospital. I was put in a much smaller ward than at Brussels with only seven beds.

They say we've all got a double somewhere, well I found mine in the next bed. It came as quite a shock. I was carried into the ward on a stretcher and lifted into bed next to this other soldier; it felt very strange looking at someone else that looked like you in the next bed. The sister said,

'You're lucky finding your brother amongst all those that came in today.'

'We're not brothers!' we both replied together, his voice sounded just like mine.

'Not brother's, not twins?' she said.

The next thing she did was check the medical record sheets at the foot of the bed, and of course the names were different.

'You must be cousins then?' she persisted.

'No relation,' we replied.

We became quite famous for a short time, with other nurses; even a doctor coming in to have a look at the resemblance. The next morning they wheeled me down to the theatre where my wounds were finally stitched up. I was beginning to think they'd forgotten me!

Last night was the first night I'd had a decent nights sleep. All the time I was in Brussels I had very little sleep, especially the first week. Although I only wore pyjama trousers I found it too hot to sleep and the bed too soft. I suppose if you think about it, moving into a central heated building after living outside for over three months, it's bound to take some time to adjust to sleeping indoors. The next week went by fairly quickly, my wounds were healing up nicely and on the 8th November I was able to get out of bed for the first time.

I felt very shaky and my left leg hurt when I put any weight on it, but that was to be expected. On the 12th November I received my first letter for over a month, it would be impossible to describe my feelings opening that first letter and reading all the news from home, it's no fun writing letters and getting none in return. The effect of a letter on a soldier from a loved one raises his morale, it's his very lifeblood, he becomes a completely different person. This first letter certainly raised my spirits again after waiting so long. It was soon after the 12th November that we were moved out of our cosy little ward as they wanted our beds, and we moved into a separate building that contained about twenty beds. We were now all walking-wounded, and had been issued with our 'Blues' – a light blue suit, white shirt and red tie – the standard outfit for hospitalised soldiers. It was while recovering in this ward that I met a Canadian soldier, I watched him making belts by platting coloured cords together. He said an old Indian had taught him. He could see I was interested, so I sat down beside him and he showed me how it was done. At the time I felt a bit like an Indian with both my cheeks painted purple. I'd had a rash come out on my face, I did look a sight, but the purple ant-septic dye certainly was clearing it up fast. I didn't feel like going out of the hospital grounds looking like I did, so I went to the Red Cross office and bought two buckles and some cord. I kept myself busy for the next few days and made two lovely multi-coloured belts. I then packed them up and posted them back home to my girlfriend.

On the 19th November with eight other lads I was invited to a party, by now my face was better so I went along, not knowing where except that it was some distance from Rouen. We arrived at this lovely house in the country and were greeted by Madame Lesouef, her husband and relatives. They could all speak very good English so we had no problem talking to them. We found out that Madame was really English and had married a Frenchman after the first world war. They made us very welcome. First they took us a little walk to show us a V1 launch site, then we all played card games or just sat talking, we had a very nice meal with wine and biscuits. I hadn't had such a good time since landing in France; it was the next best thing to a party at home. We were all sorry when the truck came to take us back to Rouen. The next day I had a bath, another pleasurable event! I made it last and enjoyed every minute of it because I knew it would be the last one for a long time.

I knew my departure had been delayed because of the rash on my face, but on the 21st November the day had arrived. We were taken to Rouen railway station by truck, there we were loaded onto cattle trucks like sheep heading for the slaughter house, and I suppose if you think about it the definition isn't all that far out, for many of us wouldn't survive the winter. The only unknown factor was how many. The journey was terrible; it was very cold and wet, the draught through the slats in the sides of the carriage made it very unpleasant. The track was in a terrible condition so the train's progress was very slow, we seemed to stop every few miles. We finally reached our destination after a ten-mile ride in trucks, tired, cold and fed up. Although after a hot meal, a wash and shave we all felt much better and the billets were buildings not tents.

We found out we were in the 40th RHU (Reinforcement Holding Unit, a transit camp) at the little town of Corbie, about ten miles east of Amiens. This was the same RHU I'd spent those couple of days in at Aldershot before sailing for France. Much to my surprise I spent nearly a fortnight in this camp, the weather was mainly wet and cold, so I wasn't complaining, it was much better here than living outside with no protection from the elements. This time I knew exactly what to expect, and I wasn't looking forward to it! Unfortunately the days went by very quickly, we did training, route marches, night schemes, I even did a guard. In the beginning my left leg was very painful, but it gradually improved. I was grateful to have this fortnight to get a bit fitter before joining the regiment in the line.

There wasn't much entertainment; we spent most of our evenings in the NAAFI (Navy, Army and Air Force Institute) or at the pictures. A lot of the lads went into Amiens at night, but I couldn't understand why they'd got scratches on their face and hands the next morning. They were very secretive at first and it was some time before I solved the mystery, apparently the train didn't stop at Corbie on the way back it only slowed down to about 20 mph. Round a bend before passing through the station. This was on an embankment the only way to get off the train was jump as it rounded the bend and roll down the embankment. The only problem was the bottom of the embankment was covered in brambles and that's where everyone ended up, now I understood where the scratches came from! With my bad leg it was out of the question for me, but it didn't deter some of the lads, in fact they got quite good at it. Jumping off a train at 20 mph in the dark wasn't my idea of fun.

The day finally came for us to move on, we travelled by train to another

RHU in Belgium. It took a day and a night to reach our destination, a long tiring journey, although this time we had carriages to travel in, so we had somewhere to sit, which was much better even though a lot of the glass was missing out of the windows. The next day we collected our new kit, I remember opening the box that contained my new rifle. It was covered with grease and took several cans of boiling water before it was serviceable. The following morning we set off by truck over the border into Holland, where we spent the night in a small camp. I met up with another lad from our old company; we passed the night away playing draughts. After breakfast our own 1st Herefordshire transport picked us up and took us back to the battalion. There we split up and went back to our companies. I went back to 9 platoon, A Company, exactly the same unit as I had left seven weeks ago!

INFANTRYMAN'S WAR

WEDNESDAY 6TH DECEMBER 1944, another memorable day for me, the day I joined the battalion again.

The company were dug-in alongside a river; I was taken to my old platoon and was immediately greeted by Jack Carrol, the lad who bandaged my leg when I was wounded. I was eager to find out how many of the old platoon were left; Jack was the only one I'd seen. When I put the question to him, he told me that when they reached their objective on the day I got wounded there were only eleven of them left out of the platoon.

'We had plenty of grub that night', he said with a grin on his face. 'I think there's only about six of us left now,' he mused counting them up on his fingers.

'Bob!' someone shouted.

I recognised the voice, turning round there was the beaming face of Sparky.

'Am I bloody glad to see you!' he said, giving me a big hug.

Of course my next question was,

'Where's Taff?'

'He was wounded a few days after you,' he replied. 'He was in a cellar one night with our cooks when a German patrol put a landmine down the coal chute. He was one of the survivors, some died including the cook sergeant.'

We'd also got a new platoon commander and platoon sergeant; it was almost like joining a new unit. The section I joined were all young lads about my age, it didn't take me long to fit in.

Jim, the section leader, was a corporal, perhaps a little older than me, then then there was Simpson (Simo) the Bren gunner, Geoff (his number two) and five riflemen including me, Tom, Stan, Maurice and Ted. What I found strange was that more than half the platoon came from the Nottingham area and knew one another before joining the army. They were in the same school together or lived in the same street, it was like a big happy family and I'm glad to say I was soon accepted into the fold!

The next few days I found it very difficult adapting to living outside again after the comfort of the last seven weeks. The weather in December was very different to when I got wounded in October. After all the rain the whole area was a sea of mud and at night the temperature was dropping below freezing, making the nights long, cold and miserable. We remained in this position for the next week; this gave me a chance to get to know all these young soldiers. By the end of the week I felt as if I'd known them forever! Then much to our surprise we were relieved and moved back behind the line, not far from the little town of Weert. There the accommodation for our platoon was a big old barn with a hayloft, it felt like the Hilton after where we'd come from. We were only there a few days but it gave us a chance to clean up and do some training with tanks. The new platoon hadn't had much experience with tanks, some none at all. The reason was because of the weather and the static nature of the campaign over the last few weeks, and also because our tanks, the 29th Armoured Brigade had retired from the forward area to Helmond and Deurne. Here they'd handed over their tanks (Shermans) and were no longer under our command.

It had been rumoured for some time that our division was to be re-equipped with a new tank, the Comet, similar to the Cromwell but with thicker armour and mounting a new 77 mm high velocity gun. The change was viewed with enthusiasm by the tank crews.

By the middle of December the new tanks started to arrive, but the process of changeover had hardly started when it was interrupted by the German offensive in the Ardennes, and the brigade found itself obliged at very short notice to collect its old tanks and drive to the scene of the battle. The Battle of the Bulge – as von Runstedt's offensive in the Ardennes became known – severely upset the expected programme of regrouping of the British forces, all plans were postponed indefinitely. Meanwhile 29th Armoured Brigade took up positions along the river Meuse covering the bridges at Dinant and Givet. They did much to save the situation in the Ardennes, but it was well into January before they were released to continue their training with the new tanks.

Last night was the first night since rejoining the battalion that I hadn't had to do a guard – no guards for any of the platoon tonight either, so we decided to celebrate with a few bottles of beer. The soft glow from the hurricane lamp made the barn seem cosy and warm, a far cry from that cold desolate place we'd left behind. Our thoughts turned to our loved ones with Christmas day less than a fortnight away, for many their first Christmas away from home. Having this little rest now would almost certainly make sure we'd be somewhere in the line on Christmas day. By eleven o'clock we'd drunk most of the beer, plus our rum ration, the lads were quite merry but were beginning to settle down in the straw for the night. Our section was still going strong, except Maurice, his legs had gone and he'd got a silly grin on his face. He wanted to keep climbing up the loft ladder and jumping off, but he never managed it. Then suddenly he wanted the toilet, luckily there was one just outside the barn, a little brick building standing on its own. Two of us walked him there and left him to it, we'd had a good night and finished what beer was left before settling down for the night. One by one we dropped off to sleep in that lovely warm cosy straw, not a care in the world.

The next morning our sleep was shattered by the platoon sergeant banging on the barn door,

'You've got thirty minutes to get your breakfasts and fall in outside ready to move off!' he shouted.

Washing outside in the water trough quickly woke us up. It was about then that someone said,

'Where's Maurice?'

I looked at Stan, then Tom, and we all realised we hadn't seen him this morning.

'He must be still in the toilet!' someone remarked.

Tom opened the door and quickly stepped back holding his nose, the smell was terrible. There was Maurice sitting on the toilet fast asleep, his trousers round his ankles.

'What are we going to do with him?' someone enquired.

'Lets get him into the barn,' said Tom, as a couple of the lads lifted him off the toilet and carried him inside. Maurice woke up and stared to cry out in pain. It was then we realised what a mess he was in, he'd taken his trousers down but not his pants. There was a circular brown stain showing through his pants and to make matters worse it was stuck to his bottom, that's why it was so painful every time he moved. By now the sergeant was calling us outside on parade, the only thing we could do was pull his trousers up, put his equipment on and get him outside. This we did, and we set off along the canal path to meet up with the tanks a mile up the road. We fell in at the end of the column so that we could help Maurice along as best we could. It was a difficult mile for Maurice, although it got a bit easier by the time we reached our destination. We fell out for a ten-minute break – that was the signal for us to get cracking. We took Maurice behind a bush alongside the canal; there we took off his trousers and with great difficulty his pants, what a mess! I'd used my bayonet for many things before but never to scrape the muck off someone else's bottom! We washed him down with water from the canal, that made him jump! It was icy cold. We then dried him up as best we could and threw his pants in the canal. His bottom was red raw and looked very sore. We'd just about finished and got him dressed when the tanks arrived. The rest of the morning we practised getting on and off the tanks, also fire and movement exercises with them. I was bored to death, even so I had to smile to myself at some of the instructions we were given, I thought: they'll learn fast enough when the time comes.

The next morning as anticipated we left our cosy barn and travelled the fifty-miles up to the line. The battalion had been given the task of patrolling a section of the river Maars. A Company occupied a small village about a mile from the river; our section was billeted in the front room of a small terraced house. Also in the house lived an old lady and her ten year old granddaughter, they lived in rooms at the back of the house. It was the first time we'd been billeted in a house that was still occupied by civilians, a new experience for us, we had to behave ourselves! The rest of the day the company dug-in around the village and arranged guard duties, each section had two men standing to at all times. Our room was very comfortable, we'd got a wood burning stove to keep us warm and an oil lamp for when it got dark. On the floor we'd each got a straw mattress to sleep on, we couldn't have wished for anything better. What we didn't know at the time was that we shouldn't be spending every night here in the village. Tom and I did our two hour turn on guard early, this gave us a chance to get six hours sleep in our new billet before we all had to get ready for our first twenty-four hour patrol.

We left the village around 0600 hours; it was a bitter cold morning with a sharp frost and the temperature well below freezing. It was a good job there was a moon to help us find our way, although being our first patrol we'd got a guide, I don't think we would have found our way otherwise. It wasn't much more than a mile, but it seemed a lot farther. The Germans had flooded the low ground – which was now frozen – this we had to cross, and there was only one safe route. The next obstacle was a small river, there had been a steel girder bridge, but it had been blown. This had caused the centre section of the bridge to collapse into the water, although the sides were still above the water level.

'They don't expect us to go over that?' someone whispered.

Sure enough our guide started across, we all looked on in disbelief but also took note how he was doing it! Now if it had been something like level and in daylight it wouldn't have been too bad, but at night, sliding down the steep metal frame and then climbing up the incline to reach the other side, and this on a steel frame covered with frost and ice, we must have been mad! Much to our amazement nobody fell in and we all eventually got over safely. From the river we started to climb. Soon we could see the silhouette of a village against the moonlight – we approached with caution. When we were about 100 yards from the houses our guide told us to wait, he went on alone. We found out later that only two nights ago our lads had shot up a German patrol coming up this very same road, there were no survivors. Our guide had gone on to warn the sentry that their relief had arrived, after the event of two nights ago everyone was a bit trigger-happy. We didn't want any mistaken identity tonight. Our guide returned, the two platoon commanders had a few words and the change over went off smoothly. The platoon then took positions in various houses vacated by the last platoon.

Our section occupied a large house at the end of the main street; it had a large bay window, which gave us a good view down the street. We set the Bren gun up on the windowsill pointing towards the river. All the time we were there, night or day, one of us had to be with the gun. It soon began to get light but it didn't get any warmer, we felt better after something to eat and a hot drink. The hours went slowly by. Our main problem was the cold not the enemy. Our position was a lot better than most, we were guarding the back door to the village, not in one of the forward positions on the banks of the river, even so it was from our bay window that the Bren gunner shot up the German patrol only two nights ago. We'd explored the territory around the house, we couldn't see across the river anywhere from our position so hopefully they couldn't see us, although we didn't move about outside in daylight unless it was absolutely necessary. One thing we all caught up with our letter writing.

It must have been late afternoon because we were all awake when we heard the back door to the house open, it had got a rather distinctive creak when it was opened slowly, no mistaking that sound. Then we heard someone coming up the hallway towards us. We all froze, the Bren gun was quietly lifted off the windowsill and Simo swung it round to face the door into the room, which was slightly ajar. The movement stopped outside our door, we could hear heavy breathing, I could feel the hair on my neck standing up as I took the safety catch off my rifle. Then slowly it moved back down the hall, the door creaked again, then complete silence.

'What the bloody hell was that?' someone whispered.

'There's only one way to find out,' said Simo, moving towards the door with the Bren gun cradled in his arms. Outside it wasn't quite dark, even so we didn't hear or see anything, whatever or whoever it was had completely disappeared into the night. At least it gave us something new to talk about; I think everyone had come to the conclusion that our visitor wasn't human, although none of us had seen any animals wandering around. I thought to myself, well we shall never know, how wrong I was. The remainder of the night passed off without incident, in another hour our relief should be here. I was looking forward to getting back to our own billet and thawing out in front of that lovely wood stove. I'd just finished my hour on the gun and was waking everyone up for stand to when that bloody door started to creak again. Everyone moved into the bay window, faced the door and listened, sure enough we heard something moving down the hallway towards us, and again it stopped outside our door, then silence. We could hear it breathing, but it didn't move. How long we waited I don't know – it seemed forever – you could feel the tension building up second by second. The door slowly began to open; the only light we'd got was from the moon shining through the window. Suddenly a white hairy face appeared round the edge of the door, then disappeared again just as quickly.

'What was that?' some one asked.

'It's only a bloody goat,' replied the corporal, a notable sigh of relief in his voice. We all had a laugh about it after, but it wasn't quite so funny at the time.

Our relief duly arrived and the changeover took place without any trouble. There were a few quips about,

'Don't forget to milk the goat!' but otherwise we arrived back safely in our billets within the hour and had soon got thawed out in front of our stove.

Over the next six days we did two more patrols, both to the same village, but this time in houses situated on the banks of the river, a much more dangerous position, with the enemy only three-hundred yards away. Also we'd had a fall of snow and the temperature at night was falling to -7C, making it very difficult to keep warm, even in our white protective clothing.

The river was very wide at this point and the snow covering the steep banks emphasised the blackness of the water. At night it became a more sinister place, shrouded in mist so that it became impossible at times to see the far bank. Our job was to make sure any German patrols were detected before they could land on our side of the river under cover of darkness. We were sending patrols over at night when it was practical; we even brought a few prisoners back on several occasions. It was a job our platoon was never called upon to do, although we did put two snipers on a small island in the middle of the river, I didn't fancy that job either.

The last patrol we did a couple of days before Christmas brought home to me the danger we were exposed to, how suddenly you could be affected without knowing it. Our position on the riverbank was concealed amongst a group of out buildings to a large house. It wasn't too bad in daylight, but during the long nights having to remain still and alert was very difficult. It was a clear bitter cold night with a moon, visibility was very good tonight and on this bright snow covered landscape our white snow suits gave us excellent camouflage. Two of us were on guard at all times throughout the twenty-four hours: that meant two hours on and four off. I'd done guards in some funny places, but never inside a chicken pen in someone's back garden before. It was an impossible situation; the chickens were still in there, about twelve of them on a perch above my head. I had to keep very still – if I didn't they started to squawk and flap their wings. Even so, the shed gave me a lot of protection from the bitter cold wind and a good view across the back gardens of the other houses. My last two hours on guard slowly came to an end – Simo was my relief – he hadn't been in the chicken pen before and his eyes lit up when he heard the chickens on the perch,

'Christmas dinner,' I heard him mumble as I made my way back to the house. My hands and feet were frozen. Much to my surprise I found Tom curled up fast asleep on the stone floor in the kitchen. I thought to myself he'll freeze to death on that floor and tried to wake him up, I couldn't! I fetched Stan, he woke the others and we carried him into the other room and laid him on the carpet. He was curled up, his knees under his chin and we couldn't straighten his legs out. He was virtually frozen stiff. I'd never experienced anything like this before. There was no panic everyone took it in turns to massage his limbs as vigorously as possible until eventually he started to moan. Everyone heaved a big sigh of relief but it was some time before we got him on his feet walking round the room, he was in terrible pain, especially in his toes. It was a long time before his circulation was restored to normal. I dread to think what might have happened if I hadn't found him when I did!

Before our relief arrived the Germans brought up a Goebbels Wagon – a loudspeaker unit – and proceeded to play us Christmas carols. It appears there was still a little humanity left in this war after all.

Our patrol over, the platoon assembled at the edge of the village for our return journey, it had been the coldest night we'd experienced of the winter so far, everyone was eager to get moving so that we could get a hot meal and thaw out in our warm billets. Although cold and tired we were all in a cheerful mood and determined to have a good Christmas day. We'd done our Christmas shopping: we'd got nine chickens and plenty of apples and onions.

The look on the old woman's face when we got back to our billet and handed over our spoils was worth all the hardship of the last twenty-four hours. The tears ran down that wrinkled face, Simo put his arms round her and gave her a hug. I've often wondered how they'd survived those five years of German occupation, all the able bodied men had been shipped to Germany to work in the factories along with most of the food they'd produced. She didn't seem to have any food in the house at all; there was a vegetable garden at the back of the house and a goat they kept for milk. I think our little help was appreciated.

While we'd been away the Christmas mail had arrived, so after our breakfasts we settled down around the stove and opened our letters and parcels. Understandably we felt a bit homesick at times like this and would have given anything to have been home with our family and friends. It was my second Christmas away from home, so for the time being this was my family, all the lads in this small room, somewhere in Holland.

Christmas day arrived, cold and frosty, the warmth from the stove made our small room very pleasant to come back to after doing your turn on guard. Under the circumstances we had a marvellous Christmas dinner, the old lady did us proud! She cooked us three chickens with soup, onions and potatoes followed by a chocolate pudding. The army dinner was bread, cheese and jam with a promise of a proper Christmas dinner later in the month!

Christmas day ended for me outside, on guard, looking up into a starry sky over a cold white landscape.

Two days later we pulled out of the line for our Christmas break, it became a little emotional saying good-bye to our Dutch landlady and her grand daughter, we had to reassure her the Germans weren't coming back and that some other unit would take our place. There was fear in her eyes as the platoon assembled in the street outside, then our last wave as the column quietly moved off. It was understandable why she was concerned, after all the Germans were only a mile away. Like many other incidents I've often wondered what happened to them after we left.

A few miles behind the line the battalion settled down in and around a small town, the name of which has long been forgotten. Our company were billeted in a large monastery near the town. It was a massive building, four stories high, A Company occupied the whole of the top floor in one large hall. There was a small stage at one end with an organ against the wall, but the most essential piece of equipment in that room was the largest cast iron stove I'd ever seen. It wasn't long before the crackle of burning wood filled the room, there was a good supply of logs, so within the hour the sides of the stove began to glow red in the failing light of the winter afternoon. Alongside the stage was a door leading to the monks' quarters, strictly out of bounds to us. It was soon dark and the only light we'd got was from home made paraffin lamps. We wrote letters, played cards and finally settled down to an uninterrupted nights sleep, the first for some time. The following day we had our Christmas dinner, only three days late so I suppose we couldn't grumble! There was plenty to eat and it was cooked well, the main course was turkey with pork, potatoes and peas, followed by a big helping of plum pudding. We also had two bottles of beer, fifty cigarettes, an apple, a pear, an orange and a packet of sweets. Where they'd acquired the oranges from I don't know – I hadn't seen one for years!

After dinner we went to a concert party given by the divisional theatre group, it was a very entertaining afternoon, something we really appreciated but hadn't expected, it helped us to relax and unwind after the tensions of the last week. With it snowing outside the day ended for us very appropriately with Jack Carrol playing 'White Christmas' on the organ.

On the 30th December I was picked with eleven others out of the company for guard duty at battalion HQ. This was no ordinary guard, we were each issued with a new uniform and given the whole day to prepare. That meant *Blanco*ing belt and gaiters, polishing boots and brasses, and also making sure your rifle and bayonet were spotless. The next morning we fell in outside company HQ to be inspected by the company commander, the whole company were watching from a distance. The major walked along the ranks inspecting each one of us in turn, he then picked the two men he thought had got the smartest turnout. No one was more surprised than me when I was one of those chosen. We were dismissed and returned to our billet, while the rest of the guard went by truck to battalion HQ to complete their guard duties. I was now excused all duties for the next two days. The rest of the platoon gave me some stick with a few choice words I couldn't repeat here. I had the last laugh though, when they had to get up the next morning and go out training in the snow, I stopped in bed! For the next week we did training from first light until our midday meal, it was quite hard work in the snow-covered countryside. After our meal the afternoons were free time, it gave us a chance to catch up with our letter writing, reading or playing cards, which was one of our favourite pastimes.

About a week later, just before we fell out for the day the sergeant major warned us not to forget that the Company Commander was holding a full company inspection the next day.

'Get your rifle and equipment cleaned up this afternoon, you've got plenty of time, so I don't want any excuses tomorrow,' he shouted.

After more snow in the night we woke to a clear cold morning, after breakfast we got ready for the inspection parade. The dress was 'Battle Order', which meant steel helmet, rifle and bayonet, belt with small pack and ammunition pouches, in other words dressed for action. The whole company lined up in the monastery courtyard, the three rifle platoons, now all at full strength and company HQ a total of 110 men. Each platoon was inspected in turn by the Major and the platoon commanders. He then addressed the whole company and congratulated us on our turnout. Ten days ago when we arrived here, as you can imagine we looked a bit like, Dad's Army. Today I must admit we looked pretty good in our new uniforms and scrubbed equipment. What happened next came as a complete surprise to everyone, the three platoon commanders then picked out the best turned out soldier in their respective platoons, the reward for those chosen was three days leave. When my name was called out as 9 platoon's candidate it came as a complete shock, I couldn't believe my luck. I didn't know where we were going but I would certainly make the most of it.

The following morning I went training with the rest of the platoon as usual, but after our dinner I got changed into my best battle dress, put my toilet requisites in my small pack and went to join the rest of the lads that were going to the rest camp with me. As the truck moved out of the courtyard the lads leaning out of windows gave us a noisy send off with whistles and a few unprintable remarks. It didn't take us too long to reach our destination; the rest camp was situated in a fairly large Dutch town in modern school buildings. Our dormitory was on the second floor, the room held twelve single beds complete with mattress, pillows and blankets and the whole building was central heated, what luxury! In the dining hall we'd got Dutch girls to wait on us, with four meals a day, there was also a separate canteen where we could get tea and biscuits or a glass of beer. A games room, reading and writing room and a large lounge. In the town there was a small NAAFI shop where you could buy all your personal requirements such as soap, toothpaste or razorblades. The theatre and cinema shows were free and there was no restriction on what you did, if you wanted to stop in bed all day you could. All this and about a dozen Dutch girls looking after all your needs … well, nearly all! If only I could stop here for the rest of the winter. I think for me the one thing I really appreciated was the female company. After living for so long in such a close all-male environment it was so nice just to sit and talk to a Dutch girl. In the evenings the girls came into the lounge and we played games, or just sat in groups and talked. It was nice to hear their experiences under the German occupation and their hopes for the future; also they were interested to hear about England and our families. Our three days leave soon went by, much too quickly for me. With the weather so cold outside it was a different world inside with central heating and a cheerful atmosphere – who in his right mind would want to leave a place like this? But unfortunately our time was up; we sat in the lounge waiting for our transport to arrive, watching the children playing on their toboggans in the snow. The afternoon went by and still no transport, so eventually we returned to our rooms and then down to the dining hall for our tea. We spent another pleasant evening in the lounge playing cards with our Dutch hosts, hoping they'd forget us again tomorrow. But of cause that was wishful thinking, the following day the truck finally arrived for us at midday. We said our good-byes and started our return journey back to the battalion.

We soon found out why they didn't pick us up yesterday, the battalion had all moved into a large barracks on the outskirts of Weert. For the next week we did six hours intensive training each day in bitter cold conditions with snow falling on most days. The training ground was about four miles from the barracks, the walk there wasn't too bad, but the return journey was hard going. Wet socks and freezing conditions don't go well together, and the cold made my leg ache. At least when the training was over we'd got a nice warm barrack room to return to and a bed to sleep in at night. There was a canteen in the camp that Tom, Stan and most of us used at night, but we also went into town to the 'Div Club' and the cinema in spite of the weather. I was disappointed that I was unable to get a birthday card for my girlfriends 21st birthday on the 17th January – although I'd tried everywhere. I knew she would understand. The battalion moved back into the line about the 20th January, I was left behind. Five out of each company had to get cleaned up, Blanco belt and gaiters and attend a parade the next day. About 0900 hours we marched into the town where we joined other regiments in a large hall. We were to form the audience for a medal presentation ceremony by Field Marshal Montgomery, it was quite an occasion and the only time I saw the commander of second army. The ceremony over we marched back to barracks, then after dark we joined our respective companies in the line somewhere on the banks of the river Maas. It was my 20th birthday and I was surprised to find cards and several parcels waiting for me when I arrived back, we had quite a party that night.

Over the next fortnight we moved several times performing the same tasks, patrols or just holding the ground, we slept in empty houses in small villages along the line of the of the river. From time to time there were fierce artillery duels, which usually started when we were trying to get some sleep. If your village was the target that night we took cover in our trenches outside.

It was about this time that Jim, our section leader, had to return home on compassionate leave and I took over the section. I immediately ran into trouble with the platoon commander, some of his orders were absolutely ridiculous. I had to parade the men for inspection at first light and he expected their boots and brasses to be polished. Everyone knows you can't polish wet boots, and we never carried metal polish in the line. In no time the whole platoon was in revolt. One snow covered night, right on the banks of the river, he crept up behind Simo the Bren gunner and accused him of being asleep on guard. Simo was furious and thrust the barrel of the Bren in his stomach and threatened to shoot him on the spot. When I arrived to see what all the commotion was about I had to separate them, they were screaming at one another. I was glad when the platoon sergeant arrived and they both listened to his reasoning. Simo was later put on 'Open Arrest'. I could never understand why this Canadian officer was in the British Army, he hated the British – well it always appeared so! He seemed to antagonise everybody he made contact with and in the end lost the respect of his men. It was only the tact and diplomacy of our platoon sergeant that held the platoon together at this difficult time. This bitter cold weather was beginning to have an effect on everyone and the job we were doing didn't help.

In the first week of February we pulled out of the line and returned to the barracks at Weert again so that we could get baths and a change of underclothes. It was while I was here that two of us out of the company had to report to the hospital in the town and go on a chiropody course. While we were on this course we were billeted with a Dutch family not very far from the hospital gate. We slept in a downstairs room and had our meals in the hospital canteen. It was supposed to be a two-week course but it had to be condensed into seven days because of the time factor. At the end of the week we had a written examination. It was hard work but I enjoyed it. Keeping away from the platoon at this time was a bonus. They'd had a rough week. Jack Carrol was held in detention for refusing to go on parade; he'd told the platoon commander that he'd come over here to fight the Germans not prance up and down on the square. He was charged for refusing to obey an order and detained for seven days. Some of the other lads received various punishments, but the least said about them the better. We sat the examination on the Saturday morning and returned to our unit in the afternoon.

We didn't have far to go. The company had moved out of the barracks into a large brick building in the town. We'd got a stove, and straw to sleep on, although it wasn't so comfortable as the barracks. The following days our hard training continued with plenty of weapon training on the ranges built by the Germans not far out of town. It was there that I fired my new rifle for the first time since rejoining the battalion. It was my third rifle of the campaign so far. The butt on my first rifle was smashed by a shell in France. It was a good job I wasn't holding it at the time. The second one I picked up, the same day from a runner who had been wounded. The bolt and breach on that one was damaged by the mortar bomb that got me. Of all the types of training we did the one I really enjoyed most of all was firing small arm weapons such as the Bren gun, the infantry mans light machine gun, the NCO's weapon the Sten gun, and my favourite, the .303 in rifle. That's why after the war I became the company armourer, responsible for the repair and maintenance of all company weapons.

Over the last week it had got much warmer, the snow had turned to rain, which had turned the landscape into mud – not very good conditions for training exercises. Then surprisingly on February 17th and 18th the whole division moved over the border in northern Belgium while they decided our next roll we would either join the northern sector with the first Canadian Army or south with the 9th US Army. At the moment we were billeted with civilians in the town of Turnhout. The whole company was in the same street, a street comprising of terraced houses running on each side of the road. It could have been in any large town in England. In our house there were five of us sleeping in the front bedroom, but the accommodation varied according to how many each house could sleep. The Belgian people were marvellous and treated us like their own sons; they soon made us feel at home.

The next morning I had another unexpected surprise, we fell in on the road outside our billet and the company sergeant major read out a list of names, about ten in all, and mine was amongst them. We were told to fall out. The rest of the company marched off on a training session. It was noticeable that all those picked were those that had been with the battalion a long time. Now since the beginning of the year people that had landed in France in June 1944 had been having home leave, but owning to a lot of sailing being cancelled because of the severe weather a lot of those due this month had been put back, including mine. As you can imagine we began to speculate, especially those lads who came over in June.

We didn't have to wait long. The sergeant major called us together, told us to get changed into our best uniforms. We'd all got 48 hours leave in Brussels; transport would pick us up at 0900 hours. Some were a bit disappointed of course, but this was the next best thing. It was only about a two-hour journey to Brussels. Our accommodation was in one of the largest hotels in the city. There were three of us in our room; we had single beds with deep soft mattresses, white sheets and our own luxurious bathroom. After our meal we went sightseeing, it's a lovely old city with beautiful architecture. I think what surprised me more than anything were the shops and arcades, they were full of things we hadn't seen in England for five years. The clothes, toys, luxury goods, even chocolates and confectionery on display in the shop windows. I can still taste those beautiful cream cakes! The only trouble was that most of the goods were much too expensive for our pocket, although

I did buy a few items, including a silk headscarf for my girlfriend. The two days I was there I spent £10. I know that sounds ridiculous now, but in 1945 that was over five weeks pay for me! After a good meal in the NAAFI we spent the evening in the cinema before returning to our hotel rather tired after our busy day. Before retiring I had a good soak in the lovely bath while I'd got the opportunity. The bed was sheer luxury – I slept like a baby. I could have stopped there all day but my two mates had other ideas.

We had a good breakfast in the dining room downstairs, then before going out on the town we went into the photographic studio in the foyer and had our photographs taken. We spent the rest of the day continuing our sight seeing; there were numerous clubs and canteens we could visit for our meals. The Montgomery Club was something special, you entered the dining hall up a vast marble staircase into one of the largest rooms I've ever seen. There was a stage at each end of the room with a band playing on both at the same time; I've never experienced anything like it before. If you walked the length of the hall you started with one melody slowly changing to whatever the other band was playing as you passed the halfway mark. The room was filled with small square tables with four chairs to each table, hundreds of them, I couldn't get over the size of the place. The room was quite full when we went for our lunch, but I remember the three-course meal was excellent. We spent the afternoon in the cinema and the evening watching a variety show in the Garrison Theatre, and so ended another full and entertaining day. After a nightcap in the hotel bar we didn't need rocking to sleep that night. We had a lie in the following morning and a late breakfast, I collected my photograph and also bought a silk handkerchief from the shop in the hotel foyer. The transport to take us back to the battalion was due after lunch at two o'clock, so I decided to have a quiet relaxing morning in the hotel lounge and write a long letter to my girlfriend Margaret. I found a quiet corner and wrote my letter – my thoughts with my loved ones. I put the photograph and the small handkerchief in the envelope, sealed it and put it in the post box in the hotel foyer; it was Tuesday 20th February 1945.

In February 1998, fifty-three years later, I opened that letter and read it again. It brought a lump to my throat and a tear to my eye as the memories came flooding back. We've still got the photograph and Margaret has still got the handkerchief, but there was something else in the letter that I'd forgotten all about, a poem I'd cut out of a magazine. The words describe much better than I could how I felt at that point in time, the belief that I would somehow survive and eventually return to my loved ones.

> *The days will not be long enough*
> *when I come home once more,*
> *so many plans and schemes I've made*
> *for happy hours in store.*
> *So many dreams to be fulfilled*
> *and wishes to come true,*
> *there will be so many*
> *lovely things to say and do.*
>
> *If we lived a hundred years*
> *it would not compensate–*
> *for all the happiness we've missed*
> *but we must bow to fate, and wait*
> *with patience for the turn that*
> *brings the end in view – somewhere*
> *in the future where the storm-clouds*
> *meet the blue.*
>
> *I am living for tomorrow*
> *we'll forget the past, in the joy that*
> *will be ours when I return at last.*
> *This is the thought that kindles hope,*
> *the faith that feeds the fire: every day*
> *is one day nearer to my heart desire.*

Our transport duly arrived to take us back to the company at Turnhout. By four o'clock I was reunited with my mates and the Belgium family. We exchanged news but they still didn't know any more about our next move. While I'd been away they'd been training hard each day with route marches, cross country runs and weapon training. Stan collected the mail. I had quite a lot including a parcel from my mother; in it amongst other things was a large piece of home cured bacon from Mom's brother. This would have been luxury back home at that time and I really appreciated the thought. The woman of the house cooked it for our supper that night, all the family joined in. They provided the eggs.

Over the next few days I began to know and like this Belgian family. There were the old mother, father and daughter, who would be in her early forties. She worked nights at the local laundry, which was very convenient for us because we only had to leave our dirty washing at the bottom of the stairs each night when we went to bed, and the next morning it appeared like magic washed and ironed just where we'd left it! These people were marvellous, and couldn't do enough for us. It wasn't until I wanted to go to the toilet in the night, which was at the bottom of the garden, that I found this old couple asleep in chairs in the kitchen. They'd given up their beds for us. Before we could do anything about this situation we received our marching orders. The division was put under the command of the First Canadian Army in the northern sector. Orders to move to the battle zone were issued to the division for the following morning. That afternoon the whole street became a hive of activity, trucks were loaded with equipment, and ammunition was issued. We had permission to test fire the Bren guns. It was like world war three had started as all the company Bren guns opened fire in the back gardens. They fired into the ground to avoid any accidents, then every gun had to be stripped and cleaned. While Simo looked after the Bren, we loaded all the magazines and cleaned our own rifles. We spent our last evening with the Belgian family in the kitchen at the rear of the house, we ate our supper together. No wisecracks or jokes tonight.

After a rather unsettled night we had an early breakfast, and formed up in the street outside our billet ready move off to rendezvous with our TCVs The whole street turned out to see us off, our family hugged and kissed us in turn. They became very emotional, the tears running down their faces, and it wasn't only the civilians that shed a tear that morning. The time finally came for us to leave these beautiful people and nowhere, not even in England would we get a better send off than they gave us, we felt very proud.

SPRING OFFENSIVE

25TH FEBRUARY 1945.

With the weather over the last week getting drier and brighter we felt that perhaps this long winter was finally over and that spring was just around the corner.

Our journey north to the battle zone from Turnhout was uneventful, we crossed the river Maas and the whole division concentrated south of Cleve. In the forward areas the congestion was even worse than in the Normandy bridgehead in the early days. Since October we had for the most part been living in buildings, sometimes barracks and convents, sometimes houses in Dutch villages that we shared with the inhabitants. But here in Germany, apart from a few isolated farms there were no buildings left, and so great was the number of troops on the ground that there seemed to be hardly room even to pitch a tent. Second Canadian Corps – under whose command we had now passed – were sympathetic, but until some more suitable area could be cleared they said we should just have to perch in the treetops!

I think at this point I should give you a wider picture of the operation we were about to embark on. The main objective in the coming weeks was to secure a bridgehead over the river Rhine, but first we had to clear the strip of land that runs between the river Maas and the Rhine. In the south it was fifty miles wide, there the Americans were pushing northward over the flooded waters of the Roer. In the north the Canadians were advancing south and east. This was the most difficult sector, it contained the northern end of the Siegfried line, and behind that were the secondary Hochwald and Schlieffen defences, also the great Reichswald Forest. The first stage of the operation had gone well. After heavy and destructive fighting Canadian and British troops had captured the towns of Cleve, and then Goch. The next stage of the operation was a series of thrusts. For this the first Canadian Army intended to use the maximum concentration of force at its disposal. All the available divisions were therefore to be deployed, each operating on a narrow front. The 11th Armoured Division found itself operating on the southern flank, and for the first time we were without our own tanks, the 29th Armoured Brigade.

Secondly, when we had previously moved in mixed brigade groups, the idea had always been that the infantry were there to support the tanks. Here in the Hochwald, however, we were to press on along crumbling roads, through country where the Germans would surely maintain a series of successive and connected positions and at least one actual line of fortifications, and this sort of thing can be done by infantry.

Thirdly we were destined to operate by night and day. We'd never set out to operate all round the clock before. We were to do so now! Finally, the battlefield was more systematically laid to waste than any over which we'd fought before. Destruction was familiar enough, but the devastated land between the Maas and the Rhine bore a different stamp. It reminded me of a battlefield in the first world war. Destruction here was continuous, thorough and universal.

The next morning we found ourselves slowly moving down a dirt track into enemy territory. It was a cold, frosty February morning. Our first night sleeping in the open again had been cold and miserable. The warmth from the sun rising above the trees in front of us was very pleasant, except that it made visibility difficult with it shining in our faces. Everyone was a little jumpy and apprehensive, which was to be expected under the circumstances. Very few had been in action before and for those that had, it had been a long time since we'd been on the offensive. It would be impossible to describe my feelings walking down that track on this lovely winters morning. I'd been in this situation many times before, but you never get used to it. The dryness in the throat, the sweat on your brow as the tension slowly increases. You know full well that something is going to happen, but you don't know when or what. You know it will be deadly, vicious and sudden when the action starts. Our section was in the lead today, which didn't improve our survival prospects. The other sections in the platoon were behind us, not on the track but in the fields on either side of us. The remainder of the company were following down the track some way back. We came to a bend in the track and slowed down, everything looked alright so we proceeded round the bend.

On the right was a derelict farm and out buildings and a burnt out vehicle in the ditch. We hadn't got to it when there was an explosion slightly behind us over the hedgerow. A shiver went down my spine, I knew what it was, I'd heard that sound before. We were in a minefield. I looked through a gap in the hedgerow and my worst fears were realised. One of the lads had stepped on a 'shoe-mine' – it had blown his foot off. There was no blood just a blackened stump neatly severed just above the ankle. He was one of the older members of the platoon; I'd known him a long time. We sat him up and gave him a cigarette.

'Stretcher bearers!'

The cry rang out as the message was passed back up the track. His war was over, he'd sleep in a warm bed tonight. The platoon sergeant was soon on the scene, he called our section leader over and gave him orders to take his section and check the farm buildings and make sure they were empty before we moved on.

'Mind where you put your feet,' he said, 'walk in single file and keep your eyes open.'

We followed Jim down the track towards the entrance to the farm, but first we had to negotiate a way round the burnt out vehicle. The ground sloped and was very muddy. I was last in the line and was carefully putting my feet in Tom's footprints when I slipped. I grabbed the side of the truck that saved me from falling down. It was then that I noticed the mine sticking out of the mud, half of it still under my boot. Lady luck was with me today! It was another shoe-mine, whether it had got a faulty detonator we shall never know. This antipersonnel mine was rather unique in that it was made of wood, like a small cigar-box with an overlapping lid. This made it difficult to detect. The standard metal detector was useless against this mine. We picked our way into the farmyard using all the hard surfaces we could walk on. If you looked carefully you could see small areas of disturbed ground. These mines had been laid in the last twenty-four hours. Alongside the path to the farmhouse was a small orchard, Stan noticed the mines first – you could just make out the three prongs sticking up in the grass. We found several alongside the path. We kept well away. These were, 'S' mines, a nasty piece of work. If you trod on one of these, nothing happened until you lifted your foot off, then there was a short pause before it shot into the air and exploded about head height. Around the explosive charge are packed over three-hundred ball bearings. I'll leave the rest to your imagination.

I followed Tom into the farmhouse; the rest of the section checked the barns. There was only the one room on the ground floor undamaged, the roof and upper floor was almost completely destroyed. The whole farm appeared to be deserted. There was a large table and a few chairs, but no other furniture in the room. On the wall above the fireplace was a large picture hanging aslant on a single nail. On the table was a German stick grenade. Before I could stop him Tom picked it up, I noticed a small wisp of smoke coming out of the handle, grabbed it off him and threw it through the window. Two seconds later it exploded!

'That was close,' Tom remarked.

'That was bloody stupid,' I replied, 'don't touch that picture either, that could be booby trapped as well.'

The explosion brought the rest of the section into the farmhouse, all they'd found were two pigs with legs missing after stepping on mines. They were in a terrible state; we put them out of their misery. We were leaving the farm when I heard a noise behind one of the outhouses; there I discovered a little goat on a chain. The circle of ground around which the goat could reach was completely barren, not a blade of grass left. I'd got a quick decision to make, leave him to starve to death, shoot him, or let him off the chain. I set him free to take his chance with the mines.

We joined the rest of the platoon and continued our way down the track for a couple of miles, no sign of the enemy. Hopefully we'd left the mines behind.

Suddenly the landscape changed from the small fields, orchards and woodland we had been walking through to more open country with large ploughed fields and areas of heathland. In front of us the ground began to rise. On the horizon about half a mile away was a village, you could see the church spire and the tops of the houses were just visible above the trees. We dug-in alongside a hedgerow facing the village. We passed the cigarettes around and wondered how much longer we'd got to wait before the cook's wagon arrived. We were getting very hungry, breakfast seemed a week away! Then in the distance the unmistaken rumble of tanks.

'I hope they're ours,' someone anxiously remarked.

Sure enough a short time later a squadron of tanks from one of the Canadian Armoured Brigades appeared and lined themselves up behind us facing up the hill. Also the rest of the battalion arrived. It was becoming obvious that we'd got another job to do before we were going to eat. The whole battalion lined up in two staggered lines, each man ten paces apart, and the two lines thirty paces apart. They call it 'orderly disorder', unusual, but aptly named. Why I'm describing this formation now is because we had never operated in this way before. This was the only time I can remember when the whole battalion lined up together to launch an attack across open ground against an enemy defensive position. We lay on the ground waiting for the signal to start the attack. First we heard the rumble of our 25-pounders as they opened fire. We counted the seconds before the whistle of the incoming shells passed overhead. Their accuracy always amazed me. Then the tanks behind us opened fire, their first target was the church steeple, a possible German observation post, in a few seconds it was completely destroyed. During this barrage we had a very lucky escape. A shell from the tank behind us prematurely exploded right above us as it left the muzzle brake at the end of the gun barrel. The turret on the tank spun round like a top, and although shrapnel from the shell hit the ground all around us, no one was hurt. The tank commander stuck his head out of the turret fearing the worst. The concern on his face turned to relief when he saw we were all OK.

'Sorry!' he called although there wasn't anything he could have done about it anyway.

Then finally the order came, 'Fix bayonets, move out.'

The whole battalion moved forward as one. The tanks crashed through the hedgerow behind us raking all the vegetation on our flanks with machine gun fire. Still no response from the enemy! Ten minutes later we were only about three-hundred yards from the village. I was beginning to sweat, the adrenaline was flowing. I thought if anything was going to happen, now was the time. The thought hadn't left my head when the first mortar bombs dropped right in front of us. The line held firm, no one hit the ground. It just continued to move forward, completely disregarding the mortar bombs. I shall never forget the courage those young men showed that day. Our platoon was right on the left of the line, so we weren't in the worst position, the centre section was sustaining the most casualties, but still the line held. As one fell to the ground another from the second row took his place, and so the drama continued. The intervention of our 25-pounders finally stopped the mortars, and the charge went in. The tanks smashed through the wire followed by the infantry. We didn't go into the village but went down the left flank to give protection from that side if required.

The enemy had withdrawn, the village was completely deserted, the trenches and defensive positions empty. That suited us fine, our job was done. What buildings were left standing the tanks proceeded to flatten. We dug in on the left flank just beyond the village, the rest of the company to our right. After dark our meal arrived (I've never known a meal taste so good), also trucks carrying petrol and tank ammunition. We hadn't fired a shot! Once we'd consolidated our position, one of our other infantry battalions with tank support passed through us to continue the advance through the night. We called it leap–frogging, a successful tactic we'd used all across France. Although it wasn't late it was obvious it was going to be another cold night. The sky had cleared and the stars were shining brightly, in different circumstances a lovely evening.

We all decided we'd got to find some straw if possible to put in the bottom of our slit trenches; otherwise we would have another miserable cold night. The search began, not an easy task in the dark. After fifteen minutes we had a stroke of luck, we met someone from another platoon with his arms full of hay. He directed us to a haystack at the far end of the next field. Sure enough we found it alright, and the two of us carried as much as we could back to our position, and shared it amongst the section. It was decided we could do with some more. Tom stopped to sort out what we had bought, so Stan volunteered to come back with me. It didn't take us long now I knew which way to go, we were soon there gathering up two more bundles. We were just about ready to start back when we heard voices coming from the other side of the haystack. We stopped and listened – they were speaking in German. It was then we realised they were German soldiers doing exactly the same as we were, gathering hay! We picked up our bundles of hay and quietly slipped away into the shadows. Back with the section I don't think they believed us when we told them what had happened.

We'd all had a tiring day, both mentally and physically, so after Jim had sorted the roster out for guard duty we disappeared below ground onto our soft hay beds. We hadn't got our greatcoats now so the only thing we'd got to put over us was our gas-capes. This was one of the most underrated pieces of equipment we carried. Designed as protection against a gas attack, (thankfully it was never needed for that purpose). Its main use was as a waterproof, it had got a built in bulge at the back so that you could wear it over your pack. It was made of camouflaged oilskin with press-studs down the front and completely waterproof. Why I've described it so fully is because I found another use for it right at the beginning of the winter, which I found indispensable when sleeping out in the open. In the sitting position I pulled it over my head, back to front, and my breath warmed the air inside my own personal little tent while I slept. Condensation was a problem, but that was better than the cold. In spite of another cold night we all had a better night's sleep, the insulation given by the straw from the ground was well worth all the effort last night. An hour before dawn we were woke by Jack Carrol, to stand to. Under his arm was a one-gallon stone jar, which contained the platoon's rum ration. He went round each trench every morning when the weather was cold armed with a tablespoon and this thick dark brown liquid. He was like a mother hen feeding her young, head's used to pop up out of the ground, eye's shut, mouth's open waiting for him to administer this beautiful brown nectar. I can still taste it now after all these years, as you swallowed, it was like a fire burning deep inside, you could feel the glow running right down to your toes. There wasn't anything else that had quite the same effect on a cold morning. When dawn broke we stood down, the most vulnerable time for attack had passed. Every morning someone always asked the same question,

'Where are we going today sergeant?' the answer varied, sometimes he would say, 'Swanning,' and what that meant I never really found out. If he was in a more benevolent mood he'd say,

'Oh, just a walk in the sun.'

It was becoming obvious from yesterdays action that we were about to embark on a completely different way of fighting, engagements more like an infantry division than an armoured one. We only gained a few miles yesterday, but action from now on was going to be more like first world war battles, where every hundred yards was important to the men who gained them. The Americans once over the flooded area of the Roer were relentlessly pushing northward. The Reichswald Forest had now been cleared and during these operations. The Siegfried line had been turned at its northern end. Where the line ends near Cleve, the Canadians had put up a notice to mark the spot, close by they hung out a line of washing, also duly signposted. Thus were the ambitions of Flanagan and Allen's song in 1939 fulfilled in 1945.

By mid-morning we were on the move again heading for the town of Udem. These plans however were soon altered. The progress of the 3rd Canadian Division towards Udem was delayed by heavy opposition at Keppeln and it was not until late afternoon before the Udem defences could be engaged. Upon the situation at Udem our own time of start depended. It was 1800 hours before our division was unleashed. Consequently they had hardly started when they were overtaken by darkness. The Greys and the 4th KSLI crossed the start line and soon made their first objective. From then on opposition increased. The attack was continued with the aid of natural and artificial moonlight, and by morning – after a hard nights fighting – the railway line southwest of Udem was reached with 350 prisoners, four self-propelled guns and two tanks destroyed. We entered the town of Udem itself on the same morning. I've never seen such utter devastation: every building had been hit by bombs, rockets, or shells, and as we picked our way through the rubble we were subjected to a heavy German mortar attack, just to complete the destruction of this small German town! Also for the first time since crossing the Maas he began using his large multi-barrelled mortar against us, nicknamed by the Allies as the 'Moaning Minnie'. It was used extensively n the early days in France but we hadn't heard many throughout the winter. I think a little explanation at this point would be helpful for you to understand this fearsome weapon. It was a very mobile multi–barrelled mortar; the bombs were over twice the diameter of the standard mortar and weighing over seventy pounds each. The eight bombs were rocket propelled and fired one after the other in quick succession, but what distinguished this weapon from anything else was the noise it made as it travelled through the air to it's target. On the fins of each bomb was a siren which created a high pitched wail, the nearer they got the louder the scream became, eight together were terrifying, and finally the devastating effect of eight large bombs falling in close proximity to one another. We treated this mortar with great respect!

Today the whole platoon took cover in a large bomb crater by the side of the church. While we were there a Canadian war correspondent rolled up in his jeep and filmed us with a cine-camera. He made a few notes, then asked,

'How long does it take them to load the Moaning Minnie?'

The sergeant answered,

'About ten minutes.'

He looked at his watch and soon drove off, not wanting to be around when the next salvo was fired. Who can blame him? A short time afterwards we continued down the road till we came to our waiting tanks. We climbed aboard, one section on the back of each tank. We sat there some time awaiting orders to move out. There was still spasmodic mortar fire and one fell on the roof of the house nearest to us, it sent the roof tiles flying in all directions. Unfortunately one of them hit Stan on the knee. We all jumped off the tank, Tom gave me a hand to get Stan down – we pushed him under the back of the tank, and took cover ourselves. The next bomb fell on the back of the tank, right where we'd been sitting. It didn't do any harm to the tank, except set fire to the camouflage netting we'd been sitting on. One minute earlier and our platoon would have been short of eight men! Every day in action there are incidents like this and you wonder if your luck will hold out tomorrow. They decided we would probably get to our start line quicker on foot. First we had to get over the railway crossing on the outskirts of town. The trouble was that the enemy had a machine gun giving spasmodic bursts of fire right down the track. When we got there you could hear the gun and see tracers coming right down the lines. I'd never had to run the gauntlet before but today the whole company had to. You waited for the burst of fire to stop, then dashed across the gap as fast as you could. Fortunately we all got across safely, although one of the lads gas-cape came loose and tripped him up just as he was crossing the lines, he did the last bit on his hands and knees to the cheers of the rest of the platoon. It was now 1400 hours; we'd wasted a lot of time getting over that crossing. We hadn't gone far along the road out of Udem when we came under shellfire from the high ground to our left; we took cover in the ditch at the side of the road. By now our tanks were beginning to arrive, somehow their presence always boosted our morale. We had now reached our start line and were all wondering what job they'd got lined up for us to do this afternoon. We didn't have to wait too long to find out!

With Udem now under Canadian control the main enemy resistance seemed to be from the Gochfortzberg high ground to the northeast. As we walked along the road out of Udem, we could see the ridge to our left. It was open country, some grassland but mainly ploughed fields. Right from the road it began to rise, getting progressively steeper, until the crest of the ridge was reached about a mile away. The whole company lined up along the ditch and waited. The platoon sergeant told us A Company had got the job of attacking the ridge and holding it for at least the next twenty-four hours so that the main assault along the valley could go ahead early tomorrow morning.

'What are we waiting for sergeant?' someone enquired.

He didn't answer, he didn't need to, the answer came from five miles away.

'Everyone move out!' he called as the first 25-pounder shells hit the ground about two-hundred yards in front of us. Climbing out of the comparative safety of that ditch, up the bank into the open fields, not knowing what was waiting for you wasn't the best way to spend a sunny afternoon. With the possibility of bazooka-parties concealed in the scattered hawthorn bushes the tanks raked all the suspect places with machine gun fire, the tracers were ricocheting off the ground in all directions.

The assault on the Gochfortzberg had begun. We advanced behind a creeping barrage, the 25-pounders dictating how fast we moved. A quarter of a mile up the hill we reached the first German defences, there were bunkers dug into the hillside each holding about a platoon of infantry. All the centre sections of each bunker had been covered with logs and soil as protection against our artillery. The trouble with this system was that only a small section of trench at each end could be used to defend the position, it was also very conspicuous. When we came under fire we quickly moved behind the tanks using them as cover. A shell from the tanks 75 mm gun into the bunker soon demolished it; they didn't stand a chance, logs and soil shot in the air in all directions. We then moved in to finish the job. Invariably the survivors crawled out of the rubble and surrendered. Those that didn't were quickly eliminated. We then gathered them together, and after disarming them, pointed them down the hill carrying their white flags for someone else to look after. This process was repeated several times as we approached the crest of the hill, also there were fewer soldiers in the last bunkers, leading us to believe they'd been slipping away before we'd arrived. At this point we'd taken 120 prisoners with very few casualties ourselves. In front of us lay the crest of the hill. We moved slowly forward, but it was one of those hills where you reach what you think is the top, and it still rises again. We'd got a light reconnaissance tank with us, which moved forward to have a look over the top of the hill. We all stood and watched its progress as it slowly reached the crest of the hill. It stopped rather suddenly and the crew jumped out. They'd hardly touched the ground when a 88 mm armour-piercing shell hit the front of the turret; it then burst through the back and whistled over our heads, the red tracer glowing brightly. On the other side of the valley was a solitary white farmhouse, the 88 mm shell hit it smack in the middle and set it on fire. We looked at one anther in disbelief at the sheer velocity of this weapon! Why the crew bailed out when they did, we never found out, they retreated down the field as fast as they could. The crippled tank started to smoke and was soon a blazing hunk of metal, its part in the war over.

It was at this point that one of those incidents happened that altered the fate of our platoon – I suppose you could simply call it luck. On the right of our position was a gully, like a deep cut into this flat field, it ran to the edge of this large ploughed field and was full of hawthorn bushes and brambles. I didn't know then what an important part that gully was going to play in the survival of our platoon over the next twenty-four hours.

As we continued past the gully, just by sheer chance I happened to look back and noticed some movement amongst the hawthorn bushes. I stopped and looked again, sure enough it appeared again. Only for a second, but it was definitely a German soldier. I called out,

'Germans in the gully!'

Everyone hit the ground and faced the new threat. There was a quick exchange of orders from the Company Commander and nine platoon was given the task of clearing the gully. Eight platoon took our place and continued advancing slowly up the hill. I was the first to reach the bushes and climbed down the bank into the gully, it was much deeper than I thought! At the bottom was a small clearing. As I stepped out into the open a German soldier came through the bushes opposite, he was more surprised than I was. We were only about ten feet apart. Our eyes met and for a split second we both froze. I was the first to react, with a scream I lunged forward thrusting my bayonet towards his middle. He dropped his weapon, neatly side stepping as my bayonet brushed against his belt, then grabbed the end of the rifle barrel as it went past his body and held on tightly with both hands. By now the rest of the section arrived. What did they do? They sat in a row on the top of the bank and cheered, or made a few sarcastic remarks until one of the section leaders arrived. He levelled his Sten gun at the German and shouted,

'Bob! Move out of the bloody way!'

At that point this very young terrified soldier let go the rifle and dropped on his knees putting his hands on top of his head. Someone picked up his weapon. I got him to his feet; the tears were running down his cheeks. I thought it was fear at the time but I soon found out the reason. He led me down the gully where we found another German soldier. He was lying on the ground mortally wounded, but still conscious. It was then that we found out it was his father, the rest of the unit had escaped down the gully. I had to admire this young lad; he chose to stop with his father at the risk of losing his own life even though he knew his father was dying. The old soldier died in his son's arms a few minutes later.

The platoon dug in along the top edge of the gully. Attempts to move eastward over the top by seven and eight platoons brought down heavy fire from the enemy, who was still holding positions on the reverse slope. Now they knew where we were the mortar fire became more intense. Eight platoon were caught in the open and sustained heavy casualties. Only a handful made it back. We got below ground as quickly as possible. Someone gave the young German soldier a shovel and he set to with enthusiasm, and dug all the trenches for platoon HQ. That done, he buried his father where he'd died under a tree in the bottom of the gully.

For me, the next twenty-four hours were the most terrifying I'd ever experienced since the morning I was wounded. I'd been under bombardment many times before, but this was something different, this was persistent and continuous, hour after hour. With seven-platoon dug in over to our left, and us in the gully, eight platoon gone; we were now down to about 70 men to defend this ridge. The Germans knew exactly where we were and concentrated their bombardment of mortars and 88 mm shells into an area about the size of a very large football field. Many times throughout the night and the next day I kneeled and prayed in the bottom of that trench, and I wasn't the only one. With all the many hundreds of bombs falling all around us it seemed that it was only a matter of time before the fatal one dropped in our trench. They hit the parapet on both sides in the night – covering us with soil – we dug deeper! Hour after hour the attack continued, the only breaks we had was when they ran out of mortar bombs, then there would be a pause, and it would start all over again. In one of those breaks, I had to go forward and find our two snipers who were dug in about fifty yards in front of the gully. They'd got the unenviable task of giving us early warning of possible attack. As I crept forward I felt very vulnerable in the open after the comparative safety of our trench. It wasn't a dark night, I could see quite well. The ground was completely covered with bomb craters. There wasn't a square yard of original ground left. I moved slowly forward, quietly calling their names. There was no answer! Then I had the fright of my life when a rifle barrel was thrust in my face. I'd found my two mates, and thankfully they were both alright.

'Return to the gully at first light,' I said, passing on the platoon sergeants message. I didn't waste any time making my way back to the section.

An hour before dawn the platoon commander came round and warned us to be prepared for a possible German counter attack.

'I don't want anyone falling asleep, I know you are all very tired.'

That was an understatement! Dawn broke, my two mates had returned to the gully, and to everyone's relief no counter attack materialised.

Daylight didn't bring any relief – the bombardment continued throughout the morning more ferocious than ever, we kept well below ground as the shrapnel whistled overhead. In one of the breaks we watched our main assault go in along the valley behind a creeping barrage from our 25-pounders. From our vantage point we had a grandstand view, it gave the company the encouragement to hang on. In the afternoon suddenly everything went quiet, after an hour or so and no more bombs the lads started to get out of their trenches, stretch their legs, there were a few cheers. We'd survived!

In the early evening we were relieved by infantry of the 3rd Canadian Division. This was one place I was glad to leave; even so I fully believed that gully saved our lives. We brought the German soldier back with us, where he joined other prisoners in Udem.

We only had a short period to rearm and get something to eat, it had been thirty-six hours since our last meal. I also realised I'd smoked five packets of cigarettes in twenty-four hours, that's something I'd never done before or since! Stan's knee was swollen where the roof tile had hit him, he'd have a nice bruise there in a few days time. All the survivors of the last twenty-four hours were a bit 'bomb happy', some worse than others. For me it was a bit like being drunk, I'd never felt so exhausted. While we were on the ridge, another of our infantry battalions, 3rd Monmouthshire Regiment with tanks from the 15/19th Hussars had moved round the southern slopes of the Gochfortzberg, that's why they'd withdrawn off the ridge, they were being outflanked and would have soon been cut off. It was now our turn to pass through the Mons and engage the Schlieffen defences a few miles further up the road.

We set out on foot in the dark, with four tanks from the Hussars. It didn't take us long to pass through the forward positions of the Mons the road soon turned into a waterlogged dirt track. Just about firm enough to support the tanks. Progress was slow, obstructions had to be cleared off the track, we seemed to be waiting about most of the time. This was a fatal situation, we hadn't moved more than a mile up the track before we'd lost half the company. They'd fallen asleep one by one along the side of the road. The sergeant major had to go back and round them all up. I remember falling asleep standing up leaning against the back of one of our tanks. How long I was like that I don't know, but I had the shock of my life when it moved off and I found myself flat on my back in the mud.

Finally we got all the problems solved, the track cleared and we were on the move again. We took the lead, that's 9 platoon, the rest of the company – what was left of it – followed with the four tanks in the rear. Like last night it was cold clear starry night, visibility was good. We passed a farmhouse on our right surrounded by a hedgerow enclosing an orchard. Beyond that it was open country on either side of the track. The road began to rise from that point, and we could see some more buildings silhouetted on the horizon some distance away. We had to negotiate some fallen telegraph poles, although the tangle of wires was a greater problem in the darkness. A little further up the road I could see the features of this fairly large building in front of us more clearly. It had got a tall chimney and out buildings stretching out to the right. On the left hand side between the house and the track was another dark shape, which I couldn't identify. We were now only about 150 yards away, and although it was a cold night I began to sweat, instinctively I sensed we were walking into trouble. I turned round and called to Tom, Stan and the rest of the section who were following behind,

'Get off the track.'

As we moved to the right, there was a blinding flash and a ball of flame from the side of the house, then a rush of air like a train going through a station, as the 88 mm armour piercing shell passed only a few feet above our heads. It hit the first of our tanks coming up the track, which immediately set fire and burst into flames. We dived into the shallow ditch at the side of the track, just in time as two machine guns opened fire on us from either side of the track. Our other two sections weren't so lucky, and got caught in the crossfire from the machine guns. That shape I saw at the side of the house was the turret of a Tiger tank. What fooled me was that it was dug in with only the turret above ground, what was known as 'hull down', a very formidable defensive position! It fired three times in quick succession and the first three of our tanks went up in flames, the fourth one was lucky, he was able to reverse out of sight behind the farmhouse we had passed earlier.

What I've just described took less than sixty seconds, we soon realised we were in a desperate situation. With our tanks knocked out, the Tiger turned his attention to us. Once again lady luck, or whatever you'd like to call it, came to our rescue. He tried to bring fire down on us with his turret machine gun, but a few yards in front of our position the ground rose forming a slight ridge between the tank and us. If he fired too low it hit the ground in front of us and the rounds ricocheted into the air. If he then elevated enough to miss the ground, the rounds went six inches above our packs, frightening

87

but safe, if we lay flat on the ground and kept still. In the end he gave up. The next thing they tried was lobbing bazookas at us, he had more success with them, and we took more casualties. Although we had only been pinned down a short time really, we were beginning to think we'd soon have to make a run for it; the bazookas were slowly taking their toll. Then like many times in the past our 25-pounders came to the rescue. They blasted the enemy positions with hundreds of shells, dead on target. We were up like a shot and carried our wounded back down the track into the orchard we'd passed earlier. I helped Stan carry one of our lads; we put him across our rifles turning them into a makeshift stretcher. He'd been hit 18 times, luckily all in his legs. He survived alright, and eventually made a full recovery, others weren't so lucky. The wounded were treated by our stretcher-bearers and ferried down the track as soon as it was practical. We dug in as fast as we could in the orchard, there was a good thick hedge between us and the open country we'd just vacated, that helped us feel a little less vulnerable.

We were looking for the Schlieffen defences; well we'd found them alright! Tonight we'd been very lucky, I wasn't looking forward to going up that track against such formidable opposition tomorrow night, but I knew someone would have to do it! We settled down and tried to get some sleep, one of us awake in each trench, I did the first watch. The first hour was uneventful, then I noticed a shadowy figure moving about the orchard. It turned out to be Jack Carrol; he was going round each trench dishing out tea from a big enamel jug. Where he'd found the facilities to boil water or the ingredients to make tea was a mystery. When I asked him, he just grinned and tapped his nose with his finger and said,

'Drink it up while it's hot.'

Dawn finally came, grey and cold. We felt better after a hot meal and some sleep. The day dragged on and with spasmodic mortar fire throughout the day we didn't move very far from our positions. When darkness came our artillery started to pound the enemy defences, then those dreaded words,

'Get dressed, prepare to move out.'

Once again we slowly moved up the track, and once again those machine guns opened fire on us. We took cover in the ditch exactly as before, and the nightmare began all over again. Tonight I got completely tangled up in telegraph wires, I couldn't move, Tom helped me get my equipment off, that's the only way I could untangle myself. I'd just sorted myself out when a bomb fired from a bazooka landed straight in front of me. I caught the full blast in my face, everything went black and my eyes began to smart as if they'd had pepper thrown in them. It took a few moments to come to my senses, but when I opened my eyes, I couldn't see a thing! I think that was the most frightening moment in my life. I called out in shock and pain. Stan and one of the other lads came to my rescue and led me down the field out of danger. They took me to a Canadian medical team in an old barn, where someone examined my eyes. They said my eyes didn't look damaged and my sight would probably come back after a few hours. That reassurance made me feel a lot better, also in the barn was a hurricane lamp and I was able to distinguish between light and dark for the first time.

Eventually we made our way back to the orchard, my eyes much to my relief were improving all the time. After another failed attempt, what was left of the company were all back in their dugouts. I lost another old friend tonight; he'd been with the platoon since Normandy and had only just returned from home leave, he came from Wolverhampton. The following morning my sight had returned and for the first time I was able to look at myself through a mirror. My cheeks and eyes were red and swollen, and quite painful, but I could see alright. It would be impossible to describe the feeling of relief to be able to see again, the pain and discomfort would pass with time. The next night found us up that track again making our third attempt to breach the Schlieffen defences. We reached the wire tonight, but at great cost, and finally had to call our 25-pounders to get us out once again. Stan got hit tonight with shrapnel from a bazooka, so it was my turn to help him down the track. Luckily it was only a flesh wound in his thigh. A lot of our mates died on that field tonight. We said our goodbyes to Stan and the rest of the lads as they were taken down the track under cover of darkness to the nearest field-dressing station. The strain was now beginning to show as each morning more trenches in the orchard were empty. I began to wonder if ours would be one of the empty ones tomorrow!

One hour before dawn I awoke to the platoon sergeant's voice calling everyone to stand to, like he did most mornings. Although an attack in these circumstances was very unlikely, their position now was purely defensive. All they had to do was hold us up as long as possible so that their comrades could escape across the Rhine, and that's exactly what they were doing. The sergeant was in a foul mood, Jack Carrol had gone missing again, he was nowhere to be found anywhere in the orchard. He'd done this before, but he'd always turned up in the end. Today was no exception, just before it got light one of the anti-tank gunners in the hedgerow noticed a figure walking towards him; it was Jack returning from his walkabout. Before the sergeant could utter a word, Jack called out,

'The tank's gone, I've been up to the wire, and the position looks deserted.'

This was great news, it certainly took the wind out of the sergeant's sails. He dragged Jack off to see the company commander. Sure enough when it got light, a patrol from D Company confirmed that the whole area in front of us was clear. We found out later that on our right flank the 4th KSLI had found a way over the ant-tank ditch using a scissor-bridge, and with a squadron of Hussars had attacked the German positions from behind. This put the enemy on our front in danger of being cut off, so that's why they'd quietly withdrawn under cover of darkness last night. By mid-morning, with mixed emotions, we walked up that track for the fourth time, glad that the battle was over, but sad for the mates we had lost. It looked very different in daylight; we could see now the extent of the defences we'd been up against. Our dead were scattered on either side of the track where they had fallen. Now at last we could bury them. We dug in around the house and outbuildings the Germans had occupied, our part in this offensive was over.

On the high ground to our left the Canadians and 43rd Division were swiftly approaching Xanten. On our right 30 Corps was pushing steadily up the main road towards Wesel, while farther over still the Americans had come up in great style from München-Gladbach. Our forward units had reached Sonsbeck but that was as far as we went. The Canadians took over from us there, and the whole division came to a halt. The trouble was too many units trying to operate in an ever-decreasing space!

For the next two days the battles raged forward of our position and on our flanks, we also came under some mortar fire, but after that the action moved on leaving us alone in this desolate place. The farm buildings had been virtually destroyed by our 25-pounders. In one of the outbuildings the winter's supply of anthracite had caught fire. We soon took advantage of this wonderful source of heat to cook our meals, and keep warm, especially after nightfall. I shall never forget the bitter cold nights and frosty mornings, Jack Carrol coming round each trench at first light with our rum ration, and the utter boredom of sitting in that trench, feet froze, hour after hour day after day. After the first week everyone was getting a bit tense, arguments were breaking out, then suddenly late one afternoon the order came through for us to pull out. It was with a feeling of some relief, walking back down that track for the last time, past the three burnt out tanks with the cremated remains of their crews still inside. I would never forget the many friends I lost here.

After walking about three miles we dug in for the night in a large field. The whole area around us became a hive of activity. Artillery pieces of all sizes began lining up as far as we could see. In the next field our own 25-pounders of the Ayrshire Yeomanry lined up their twenty-four guns. These were the gunners who had come to our rescue many times in the past. It soon became obvious that we were about to witness something very special. Before it got dark around us were 48 regiments of artillery, that's over a thousand guns lined up to open fire on the last bridge over the Rhine in the town of Wesel. All German units this side of the river were now in full retreat, and heading for this last bridge.

The barrage that followed was second only to El Alamein, and lasted all through the night. To try and describe the noise and smell is impossible, the whole area disappeared under a blue haze. The cordite made your eyes smart and your throat sore, and nobody, not even the gunners had ear-muffs in those days! Then the impossible happened, I curled up in the bottom of that hole in the ground and fell fast asleep completely oblivious to everything around me.

The next morning we awoke to the good news that the division was moving back out of Germany to a rest area in the region of Diest and Louvain in Belgium. This was something few had dared to hope for and certainly not expected. The whole atmosphere in the company changed in a few minutes. The date was the 9th March 1945.

Without doubt the last fortnight had been the toughest two weeks, both physically and mentally, of the whole campaign so far. I can now appreciate in a small way what the first world war soldiers had to endure in trench warfare.

With the German army now eliminated west of the Rhine, we can now reflect on the general background of this allied victory, and console ourselves upon what has been for us a slow, miserable and costly operation. We had been fighting our way through country where no armoured division could have been expected to fulfil its natural role. We had been confronted by impenetrable forests, impassable bogs, roadblocks, mines and every form of demolition. Except as morale-boosters for the infantry, the tanks had been practically useless. The infantry as usual bore the brunt of the fighting, and the fact that we advanced at infantry pace meant we were continually on our feet. I'd never experienced such exhaustion before; at times we were out on our feet. Nor was our progress made any easier by the activities of our own troops. Operating now for the first time on German soil they set about the work of destroying towns and villages with undisguised enthusiasm, and the resulting debris frequently delayed traffic for many hours until it could be cleared. We had won this battle but now that the German army was defending the fatherland we could expect even harder battles once we crossed the Rhine.

LEFT OUT OF BATTLE

Haacht was a typical small Belgian town with its main street of terraced houses, shops and cafes. It was situated on a road junction about sixteen miles from Brussels. There was a small cinema and adjoining shop that sold chocolate and ice–creams, it was like going to the pictures again in pre-war days! Our section was billeted in a cafe, six of us shared a room on the ground floor next to the bar, we couldn't have wished for anything more convenient. The proprietors, a married couple in their thirties took us in with open arms. They were lovely people, there was also a younger sister living there, she worked in the bar at night. I think we'd got the best billet in the company, as well as being the farthest away from company HQ and the sergeant major. That had got to be a bonus! We hadn't got beds to sleep on, but we'd got the next best thing: we'd each got a sprung mattress on the floor, what luxury! After a good nights sleep the next day we spent getting cleaned up, having showers and changing into clean underwear. Last night was the first time I'd had my boots off for over a fortnight. Most nights the family cooked us some supper, and one day I remember the younger sister ironed all our uniforms, and sewed on all our new div-signs.

For the next sixteen days we trained hard, we were made up to strength in men and equipment and took our pleasures. There was time for sport and games. Competitive football games were arranged and best of all, day passes to Brussels. Even the weather was brilliant, with warm sunny days; the difference to the two weeks we had just experienced in Germany was unbelievable.

On the morning of the 24th March 1945, the day we'd all been waiting for finally arrived, the air-assault across the Rhine began. The noise of low flying aircraft brought everyone out onto the streets to witness the largest air-assault in history. Wave after wave of gliders being towed to their drop zones on the other side of the Rhine. People cheered and waved, and still the planes passed overhead. What surprised me was how low they were, then suddenly it was all over and it went quiet and peaceful once again. It took some time for the realisation of what had happened to sink in on this historic Saturday morning, but it also meant that in a few day's time it would be our turn to breakout of the bridgehead being secured by the troops in those gliders today. I can't say I was looking forward to that job very much.

The next morning we put our best uniforms on, polished our boots, and went on church parade. The service was held in the little cinema. Then after our lunch Tom, Maurice and myself decided to hitch-hike to Louvain to see our old mate Stan, who had been taken to the 101 General Hospital there to recover from his shrapnel wounds. We were in luck; the first truck we stopped took us straight to the hospital. It was a massive place, and took us ages to find the ward Stan was in. Even then it took the three of us five minutes to find him. It was the biggest hospital ward I'd ever seen, with one hundred and seventeen beds, and what made it more difficult Stan was down under the sheets fast asleep. Even when we did find the right bed we didn't recognise him, Maurice passed him by the first time. Here was a tidy, clean-shaven young man, his hair slicked back in his blue striped pyjamas. The last time we saw him he'd got a beard and a fortnights grime on his face, no wonder we didn't recognise him right away. He was surprised and pleased to see us. He said his wounds had healed nicely and was hoping to be released from hospital in a couple of weeks. We told him not to be in too much of a hurry, he was better off where he was! We had a pleasant hour together, Maurice's dry sense of humour kept the conversation going, especially when the nurses were about. When the tea arrived it was time for us to go, we said our good-byes and the other lads in the ward out of our battalion waved and wished us luck. It was only a short walk down the hill into the town, our first priority was to find the nearest canteen and get something to eat. NAAFI tea and buns tasted just the same everywhere; we had our fill and spent the evening in the cinema. I can even remember the film: Spencer Tracy in Boys Town. We then caught one of our trucks back to Haacht, arriving back at our billet at 11:30 PM, tired after an eventful day.

At the end of the main street farthest away from our cafe was a piece of waste ground the company used as a parade ground, we fell in there every morning for roll call. For the last fortnight this had been our first parade.

When I fell in there that morning I didn't know it would be for the last time. After roll call the company commander read out a short list of names, mine was one of them. We were told to pack our kit and be prepared to leave the company tomorrow morning for the Divisional Battle School near the town of Weert in Holland. We had been chosen to be Left Out of Battle (LOB). Perhaps a little explanation at this point would be helpful.

There was only one battalion of the Herefordshire Regiment, and army ruling at that time stated that if the battalion were to be wiped out in action the regiment could not be reformed. That's why this small force from the four rifle companies (about fifty men) were left LOB, so that they would become the nucleus of a new battalion should the unthinkable happen! It had been common practice at the beginning of the campaign, but for a long time now we'd never had enough men to spare to be left behind. Today over fifty years on it seems a bit bizarre, especially when so many of the old regiments have been disbanded or amalgamated.

The following morning I said goodbye to our Belgian hosts and the lads in the platoon. It was with a heavy heart and a feeling of guilt when I hugged Tom my digging in partner for so long. The tears ran down his face as I climbed aboard our transport and waved good-bye, but like he said, in the army you look after number one. There were a lot of faces in the platoon that sunny morning I would never see again.

The division had received orders that morning to be prepared to move out for the battle zone in the Wesel bridgehead on the 28th March 1945 for the final assault into Germany.

Our journey to the battle school was uneventful; it was a small camp situated about three miles from the town of Weert, which I knew quite well from previous visits. The first day we just got settled in our new billets, then the following morning we started a basic training programme. By the end of the week we were bored to death, but consoled ourselves with the fact that we were better off here than with the battalion.

On the Sunday afternoon two of us walked into town, and while we were there I decided to visit the Dutch family I'd stayed with while I was on the chiropody course earlier in the year. They were surprised to see me again and made us very welcome. They insisted we stop and have something to eat, and wouldn't take no for an answer. We had an egg with bread and butter, it was a nice change for me, I couldn't remember the last time I'd had an egg. Afterwards we sat and talked over coffee, the daughter could speak quite good English so we had no problem understanding one another. When we were leaving, we thanked them for their hospitality, and said we thought we'd spend the next couple of hours in the cinema, before walking back to camp. The daughter said she'd like to come with us, it was an opportunity to see a film she'd always wanted to see, so she came along. She couldn't have got in without an escort anyway, that was army regulations at the time. We took her back home afterwards, and she thanked us, and wished us luck in the future. Our day was spoiled by the return journey, it rained all the way back to camp, we were soaked!

A couple of days later we fell in as usual for the first parade and sensed something was wrong, there was a slight panic and a lot of activity going on. Then we were informed to pack our kit and be prepared to rejoin our battalion immediately. We loaded everything into two Bedford three-tonners, and were on our way within the hour. Nobody said why, but we knew in our hearts there could only be one reason, the battalion had sustained heavy casualties.

OVER THE RHINE

We travelled northeast throughout the day, first crossing the river Maas at Venlo. Travelling in the back of an open truck wasn't the most comfortable way to travel. As you can imagine the roads were in a terrible state, and the nearer we got to the town of Wesel, where we crossed the Rhine, the worse they became. This was the town that received that massive artillery bombardment we witnessed before we returned to Belgium. The town was completely reduced to rubble, the bulldozers had cleared a way from the bridge straight through the town and we got caught up in a queue of traffic of every description, trying to get over the river. This took much longer than anticipated so by the time we'd cleared the town it was late and so we decided to find somewhere to spend the night. We pulled into a field and set up camp. Some of us slept in the trucks, others in makeshift shelters using the tarpaulins out of the trucks. The next morning we set off quite early following a route we had got marked off on our maps. We got lost a few times and the roads were very bad in places making progress rather slow. Even so we reached our marked destination in the evening only to find the battalion had moved on. This didn't come as any surprise really, we were half expecting it, but it was a start line for tomorrow. That night we slept in wooden huts, the few remaining ones from a small German camp. This was a big mistake, the next morning we were covered in flea bites; it was a good job we didn't get undressed.

We continued our journey, gathering information as we went. What surprised me more than anything was the quietness everywhere. We didn't see any civilians and sometimes it was hours before we even saw any of our lads. We were beginning to get a bit concerned, we weren't quite sure where we were and there wasn't any sound of distant gunfire. It was a lovely sunny day, the hawthorn hedgerows were just bursting into leaf, it all seemed so unreal.

We must have covered nearly a hundred miles since we crossed the Rhine and we hadn't even found anyone out of our division yet. I never anticipated it would take so long to get back to the company, and I was worried at what I would find when I did. I was sitting at the rear of the second truck when I first noticed it, just a speck in the sky. We were travelling down a long straight road at the time, but my eyes were fixed on the aircraft that had banked towards us and was now approaching us very quickly straight down the road from the rear. A few seconds later and there was no mistaking that fixed undercarriage and inverted gull wing, a Junkers 87 dive bomber. By now every one was watching it, I shouted out a warning and in seconds the trucks screeched to a halt and everyone baled out. What happened next I still can't explain. I remember racing across the field trying to get as far away from the road as possible. I turned round just in time to see the bomber pass over the trucks – it didn't fire a shot. If it was only trying to scare us, it succeeded. It was then I realised I was on my own; everybody else had gone to the opposite side of the road. I watched the plane disappear into the distance, then slowly walked back to the trucks, but in between the road and me was a hawthorn hedge and an eight-foot high chain link fence. How I got over that fence I'll never know, I tried to climb back but couldn't in the end I had to walk along the hedgerow until I came to a gate leading into the road. All I can remember is jumping out of the truck, and the next minute I was racing across the field. It's amazing what fear and a surge of adrenaline can do. The excitement over we climbed back on the trucks and continued our search, and for the first time met a small convoy of trucks carrying our divsign, 'The Black Bull'. We asked where the Herefords were and they gave us a map reference, which turned out to be a small village called Schlusselburg about ten miles away, near the river Wesser. It didn't take us long to reach the village, the trucks dropped some of us off; the rest went on to their own companies further up the road. In the centre of the village were a few of our trucks parked a the side of the road. The drivers were sitting on a wall drinking tea, we went over to find out where A Company was, and were surprised when they told us they were on the other side of the river. Apparently they were ferried over there yesterday to protect the Engineers who were surveying a bridging site nearby. The good news was that they'd found a better site about a couple of miles downstream at Stolzenau, and our lads were being brought back over the river later today. All we'd got to do was sit tight and wait for them to return to the village. I settled down on the front steps of one of the houses facing the river with a mug of tea I'd scrounged from one of the drivers. I noticed two of our lads come out of the house opposite. I think they'd been up in the loft having a sleep. They hadn't left very long when I noticed smoke coming out from under the eaves. Then a woman clutching a child came screaming out of the front door. There wasn't anything anyone could do; the house was made of timber with an attic full of hay for the cattle. In minutes there wasn't anything left, I've never seen a house destroyed by fire so quickly. There was a little lad, he'd be about ten years old who kept dashing into the house trying to save some of the furniture, he managed to rescue a few chairs, but very little else. One of the onlookers had to grab him in the end – his attempts were becoming suicidal. He struggled for a time, before collapsing on the floor the tears running down his smoke blackened face. If there is a moral to this story, it must be that if you smoke in the hayloft, make sure your cigarette is out before you throw it away!

After all the excitement, we settled down again wondering if the fire had been an accident or deliberate, nobody seemed to know who the two soldiers were, so we shall never know. Then suddenly we were reminded there was still a war on as two German planes roared overhead heading for the bridge that was being constructed at Stolzenau. They strafed and bombed the site and quickly disappeared over the wooded hillside beyond the river. No sooner had the enemy planes disappeared than two of our fighters arrived on the scene. Unfortunately they couldn't stop with us for long, because of the distance they'd had to come. It was a very frustrating situation for the engineers working on the bridge, for no sooner had our planes gone, when the Germans were back again. This happened several times over the next couple of hours, even the onlookers were getting frustrated and opened fire on the enemy planes with any small arms weapon they could lay their hands on. Then the Germans luck ran out, four of their planes arrived at the same time as two of our Tempests. Three were shot down immediately, the fourth turned and ran with a Tempest hot on his tail, but before our fighter could open fire the German pilot bailed out. All this happened right in front of us, the pilot landed about three-hundred yards away and was quickly rounded up. By now we'd got a 'cab-rank' of planes reaching the bridging site and beyond, so all German planes in the area were soon destroyed. Unfortunately this didn't solve the engineers' problems. The bridge was sill under persistent machine gun fire, shelling continued throughout the day. A number of the pontoons had been damaged and the approach roads partly wrecked. The engineers had pressed on gallantly, but their casualties mounted at a disturbing pace. It was decided until the bridgehead could be appreciably enlarged little progress with the bridge itself would be possible.

By five o'clock, word came through that A Company had been ferried back across the river. Understandably I started to get a bit apprehensive, which of my mates were still alive, had Tom and Maurice survived? My questions would soon be answered, I could see them coming up the lane towards us. They looked tired and with a weeks growth of beard on their faces it was difficult for me to recognise them. I started to walk towards them and as they got neared I could see Jim our section leader followed by Simo, the Bren-gunner and his number two, but no Tom or Maurice. Simo, grinning all over his face shouted a few choice remarks when he saw me.

'Tom's alright, he's behind somewhere,' he cried, he anticipated what my next question was going to be. Tom and I met on that little lane, neither of us said a word, we threw our arms around one another, I was too emotional to say anything. I'd feared the worst when he wasn't with the rest of the section. Eventually I asked,

'What's happened to Maurice?'

'He's alright, the lucky dog,' Tom replied, 'he's landed himself a good job looking after prisoners, we've been rounding them up by the hundred this last week.'

We walked slowly back up the lane to the village, and after a hot meal we settled down with the rest of the platoon for the night in one of the houses. We sat on the floor our backs against the wall and shared a cigarette, it was there that Tom described the battle that had taken place on the 1st April 1945, where so many of the company had died trying to capture the Teutoburger Wald!

Although I took no part in this action I think it's right for me to tell you about this event if only in memory of all my comrades that died there. I'll try and describe the battle of the Teutoburger Wald as told to me by the survivors, and also the more overall picture from divisional HQ reports.

On 31st March 1945 nothing occurred to halt the advance until 1900 hours, when the leading tanks reached the Dortmund-Ems-Canal. Here again all the bridges had been blown, but with the magnificent defensive position afforded by the water barrier and the precipitous wooded slopes of the Teutoburger Wald beyond it, the enemy wouldn't lightly surrender such a marvellous defensive feature without a fight. The prize for the victor would be the Westphalian Plain and the local metropolis and communication centre of Osnabruck. The site for the bridge across the canal was to be at Birgte. During the night, 3rd Royal Tanks were ferried across the canal by means of a ferry the Germans had left intact. This squadron with men from the 4th KSLI would form a bridgehead, and then the 1st Herefords with tanks from the 2nd Fife and Forfar Yeomanry would pass through them and execute an assault on the ridge tomorrow. The next morning the engineers worked well and the bridge was completed by 1430 hours, but the assault was unable to proceed for another two hours because the exit roads from the bridgehead were under mortar and machine gun attack from the densely wooded hillside. Finally the company disembarked from their TCVs. The plan was simple, the company would clear the woods in their sector to the top of the ridge, then go down the reverse slope where the TCVs would pick them up again. Well, that's what they were told, unfortunately the German defenders had a different plan! To start with everything went fine, although it was hard going up the steep slope, they didn't meet any opposition. Then suddenly the leading platoon was confronted by a vertical rock face, stretching in each direction as far as they could see. They came to an abrupt stop, and soon the remainder of the company caught up, everyone wondering how they were going to overcome this problem, nobody had said anything about rock climbing!

Unknown to our company, the enemy had carefully planned an ambush and were concealed in the undergrowth on top of the rock face. When the action started it was deadly and ferocious, our lads never stood a chance. With grenades and sub-machine gunfire from such a dominating position we took heavy casualties. Although the survivors fought back gallantly they had to quickly retreat into the trees. This dense plantation must have saved many lives. They took cover as best they could, and in the next hour had to repel several counter-attacks. Most of these attacks were led by a big German sergeant with the SS insignia on his black steel helmet. These attacks were quite costly to the Germans, but this sergeant was most illusive and always seemed to get away. Eventually, greatly out-numbered, they withdrew down the hill carrying their wounded; it had been a bad day for A Company. I was never able to confirm how many were wounded that afternoon, but a lot of familiar faces were missing, including my old mate Jack Carrol, I bet he put up a good fight. His name never appeared on the battalion Roll of Honour (which can be found at the back of this book) at the end of the war, so he must have survived, although I never saw him again. Twenty were killed that afternoon, twelve other ranks, six NCOs and two officers, which included our Canadian platoon commander. There were also dozens of narrow escapes, two out of our platoon are worth a mention. The first had a bullet go through the front of his helmet, cut a groove across the top of his head, before blowing a large hole in the back. The blow knocked him out, and he fell flat on his face, with the blood running down his face. Everyone thought he was dead, especially when they saw the large hole in the back of his helmet. About 15 minutes later, imagine the shock he gave his mates when he sat up, his face covered in blood and demanded to know where he was. Other that a bad headache for a few days he survived.

Harry was a quiet unassuming soldier, what happened to him on April Fools day was no joke. Some might say it was his unlucky day, I thought he was very lucky. A sniper fired at him through the trees, in that same split second Harry turned his head. The bullet, which would have hit him between the eyes, went straight through the bridge of his nose, shattering the bone, bad enough, but it still saved his life. He'd never have a nosebleed to match that one again! I'm glad to say he made a full recovery, the only difference, now he'd got a slightly crooked nose. Although there was another development as the months went by, we noticed he only perspired on the one side of his face, the sweat stopped right down the centre of his brow, nose, upper lip and chin. Harry was a bit sensitive about this strange phenomenon, one of the more witty members of the platoon suggested his mother must have conceived halfway in the greenhouse. A remark Harry didn't appreciated very much, although generally taken with good humour. The Herefords took no further part in the battle for the Teutoburger Wald.

Materially the most profitable operations of the 1st April 1945 were those of 29th Armoured Brigade Group on the west bank of the canal. The villages of Bevergern and Saerbeck were cleared and fifteen guns were knocked out or captured.

There were two good roads over the Teutoburger Wald, the main road from Munster to Ibbenburen and the route that winds up the hill from Brochterbeck to Holthausen. These were about five miles further southeast from the bridge at Birgte. On 2nd April 1945 the attack on the Teutoburger Wald resumed and 159th Brigade were tasked with clearing the woods westwards to the summit. This operation was to be carried out using 3rd Mons and 2nd Fife and Forfar Yeomanry in support. Attacking up the densely wooded slopes they reached the summit at one point, but any attempt to go further met fierce opposition. The enemy originally composed of two companies in the area but had continued to reinforce them overnight until finally we were faced with no less than seven. These were troops from an NCO training school at Hanover, and very tough they were!

Two attempts to dislodge them failed with the 3rd Mons suffering severe losses, despite the great gallantry of Corporal E.T. Chapman, who for some time engaged a considerable force of the enemy on his own and killed and wounded a large number of them. In my recent research I found out, for this brave performance he was awarded the Victoria Cross.

Meanwhile, 15/19th Hussars were to advance along the road which skirts the southern edge of the escarpment, occupy Brochterbeck, and explore the possibilities of mounting an attack up the hill from there. While one squadron was blasting it's way into Brochterbeck, a village which showed no inclination to put out white flags, the remainder of the regiment turned northward and proceeded to assault the pass in true cavalry style. Making full use of the pace of the Comets, the Hussars charged up the long winding hill. By 1130 hours they were firmly established at the top. The speed of the attack, so surprised the defenders that not one tank was stopped, even though they were fired at all the way up the hill. To exploit this success, 23rd Hussars and 8th Rifle Brigade were ordered to pass through 15/19th Hussars and take the little town of Tecklenburg. Things didn't quite go according to plan. The town was stubbornly defended, the civilian population, so it was said, joined in the fighting by the side of the soldiers. It was evening before the place was cleared, by then it was so congested with rubble and smashed vehicles that the remainder of the division had to abandon this route and follow the lower road through Brochterbeck and reach Tecklenburg from the south.

Next morning on the 3rd April 1945, the Germans counter-attacked and forced two companies of the Mons from their dominating position, leaving one company on top of the ridge. 3rd Mons fought back strongly and took seventy-five prisoners, but it was evident by now that they could not both clear up the Teutoburger Wald and continue the advance. During the afternoon of the 3rd April 1945, one battalion from 131st Infantry Brigade attacked and recaptured the dominating position lost by 3rd Mons in the morning. The Germans were caught between the new attacking battalion, and the company of Mons that was holding its original position on top of the ridge. Some two companies of these German NCOs were killed almost to a man, and this allowed 3rd Mons to be relieved. It was however not until three days later that this dominating feature was finally cleared.

The 3rd Monmouthshire Regiment had now fought their last battle, after many bitter encounters they had suffered cruel losses, their casualties to officers since D-day now stood at well over 100 percent. After this latest battle they could hardly have been expected to make any further effort for some considerable time.

They were replaced a few days later by the 1st battalion Cheshire Regiment. To describe our advance into Germany as a 'Breakthrough' would be a bit presumptuous. Breakthrough, which means a violent penetration of a defensive position, followed by a period of plain sailing – in this sense the advance into Germany was certainly not a breakthrough, we weren't only held up by demolitions, but by enemy forces ready to fight hard battles in defence of positions held. The defence of the Teutoburger Wald, which I have just described, is a good example. The German army was still a well disciplined force and not ready yet to roll over and start waving white flags, even though he was now operating so far inside his own country that the thought of planned withdrawals must have seemed a mockery. Sooner or later you reach a stage when every retreat becomes a defeat. He was now being hit hard and relentlessly on all fronts. The Russians were approaching Berlin, the Americans had reached Hanover and Brunswick, the Canadians and the British were sweeping across the Westphalian Plain heading towards Hamburg. How many more weeks it would take before victory was ours, no one knew, but we all felt at last the end was in view. I didn't write many letters in April, my time was otherwise engaged, but recently looking through my old letters to Margaret I found one I wrote on the 11th April 1945 and inside was a little poem, which I thought was very appropriate.

The goal in sight, the end in view,
These cheering words impart,
Courage to the weary soul and comfort to the heart,
Goading us to fresh endeavours in the coming days,
Giving us the needed strength to face the final phase,
To fight the next big battle,
And win the last great bout,
Casting off forever every thought of fear and doubt,
The hardest task is lightened,
Hope and faith, are born anew,
When having suffered and endured,
We see the end in view.

The End in View – *Anon.*

THE FINAL ASSAULT

It was the morning of the 7th April 1945, the day following my return to the company, after being left out of battle. The weather was good, a lovely spring morning, not a sound of battle anywhere. The company were waiting for the TCVs to pick us up. Looking around it was then I fully realised how many familiar faces were missing.

'Where's Billy Smith?' I enquired.

Tom shook his head.

'Dead?'

'Yes' someone answered.

Anyone will tell you that you spend seventy-five percent of your time in the army hanging about; now Billy Smith had always been a cheerful character, always smiling, always singing, we were going to miss him. Like this morning for instance, he'd soon have had everybody singing. I'd forgotten how much we used to sing in those days. Eventually our transport arrived and we set off upstream. With work on the bridge at Stolzenau suspended, 159th Brigade crossed the river by courtesy of the 6th Airborne Division's bridge at Petershagen some fifteen miles up river. The 1st Cheshires – our replacement battalion for the 3rd Mons – arrived last night, strengthening our brigade considerably, but with three more major rivers to cross we were also entrusted with the 1st Commando Brigade. This gave us the extra infantry required to tackle the major rivers like the Aller and especially the river Elbe. Once over the river we turned north heading back down stream again. The enemy's position was centred on the village of Leese, the Commandos first task was to relieve the two companies of the 8th Rifle Brigade, who crossed the river at Stolzenau two days ago, to form the bridgehead for the ill fated bridge. The evacuation of these two companies was only accomplished with considerable difficulty, and the assault on the Leese defences was soon pinned down. It was then called off entirely in favour of a flank attack by 15/19th Hussars and 1st Cheshires – but they were delayed reaching their objective by German infantry. So it was decided to soften the target area overnight and attack at first light. Everything was thrown at the German positions, mortars artillery, but the most spectacular display was from our rocket firing Typhoons. Even the tanks of the 23rd Hussars on the west side of the river joined in the bombardment. We took no part in this battle, after travelling a few miles down river we turned east; our objective today was the town of Loccum. We met up with our tanks, the 2nd Fife and Forfar Yeomanry, leaving the TCVs behind. This was my first encounter with the Comet, our new tank; it looked good, low slung like the Cromwell but with a very impressive long-barrelled 77 mm gun. Also reputed to have the Rolls Royce Merlin engine, which made it much faster than any other tank in service, an asset for any advancing armoured division. The battle for the town of Loccum was fast and furious, at least seven 88s were knocked out before the town was taken. A Company only played a minor roll in this battle, but I vividly remember one incident. We were advancing across a rather rough ploughed field, when three German soldiers about two-hundred yards in front of us dropped to the ground and lay still. I turned to Simo our Brengunner, who was walking alongside, and said,

'Give them a burst.'

Although he fired from the hip, he was bang on target; two of them immediately sprang to their feet, hands high in the air, the third lay still. I don't think any of us were quite prepared for what we found when we reached them. The first thing we noticed was a pair of white silk knickers – the unlucky soldier was a woman. She was wearing a skirt and dark silk stockings, instead of trousers. Simo's fire had blown her kneecap off, it looked pretty bad. She never made a sound, not a murmur, although she must have been in terrible pain. The two men were wearing red-cross armbands, but they were also carrying pistols. This annoyed me; I pointed to the red-cross symbol, then the gun, and thumped him in the chest with my fist. He was very lucky he wasn't shot on the spot. After the losses of the 1st April the mood of the company had changed. One individual in the platoon who lost his mate in that battle went berserk, it was some time before he could be left anywhere near any prisoners on his own. I felt much happier when we dug in that night, my first battle over and my old mates around me once again.

The following morning we were on the move early heading for the river Leine, a tributary of the river Aller, which was about twenty miles east of our present position. We rode on the backs of the Comets. To the north of us the Commandos and the Cheshires had overrun the Leese defences, the village was completely destroyed. We pushed on relentlessly, having to fight our way through one village after another. We just hung on tight as the tanks raced on, avoiding any major roadblock by charging down back gardens between the houses. Travelling at 40 mph it destroyed everything in its path, shed, greenhouses, fencing flew in all directions, and so did the defenders. They'd never experienced a thirty-five ton tank charging at them at that speed before. We were through the village in minutes. They must have wondered what had hit them, what with the noise the tanks were creating and the rattle of the turret machine guns, it was utter chaos! I don't know who was the most scared, the enemy, or us hanging on the back of the tanks. The 15/19th Hussars and the 1st Cheshires on our left occupied Schneeren and Eilvese after clearing a well-prepared defensive position between the two villages. We then passed through them and captured the small town of Laderholz, the defenders; mainly determined bazookamen concealed at the side of the road gave us the most trouble. Usually the first four tanks in the column carried no infantry, for obvious reasons. On this occasion the bazookaman fired at the third tank from a house situated near the road. Fortunately for the tank, the bazooka hit the toolbox mounted on the side of the tank, doing no serious damage. The tank immediately stopped, swung the turret round and stuck the 77 mm gun through the window and fired, killing everyone in the room. I think at this stage of the campaign the majority of tank casualties we were getting were from the bazooka. In the hands of determined men they were a very effective weapon, even though the bazookaman was invariably killed afterwards. Their philosophy was simple; it was well worth the loss of one man and a very cheap weapon for a very costly weapon like a tank, and possibly the crew as well.

We finally reached the river Leine in the late afternoon near the town of Niederstocken, both here and at Holstorf the bridges were blown, and for the second time we had to cross a river by courtesy of the 6th Airborne Division the following day at Neustadt. On the left of the Second Army front, progress had been slow and resistance tough. Even our second column to our left, 29th Armoured Brigade were meeting more resistance than we were, and beyond them the Guards Armoured Division was having a very tough time. But on the extreme right where the Americans were now entering Brunswick the way was much easier. This seemed to indicate that the German armies in front of us appeared to be pivoting northwards and anti-clockwise towards the river Elbe.

After crossing the river Leine we advanced in a north-easterly direction following the route taken earlier by 15/19th Hussars and 1st Cheshires. When they'd reached their objective, we passed through them and fought a stiff battle at Schwarmstedt, a village just a few miles from the river Aller.

In attempting to cross the Aller here, we were a little off our beat, for the route which we had been ordered to take was about ten miles up river at Winsen. But only two miles up the road the bridge at Essel was still intact, it's seizure was too good an opportunity to miss. After the capture of Schwarmstedt we dug in across the main road and consolidated our position. Tom and I dug our trench in the grass verge giving us a good field of fire up the road towards the river. The defenders of this large village had fought a stubborn battle but had been crushed by sheer power, consequently the whole village was now burning furiously, not many houses would be left standing by nightfall. The smell from the burning flesh of the dead cattle and the smoke from the houses cast a thick cloud over the whole area, making visibility no more than a few yards in places. During the battle we were clearing some out buildings to a farm when I had to climb over what I thought was a pile of debris. But under that debris was a dead cow and my leg suddenly broke through the animal's rib cage right up to my knee. What a bloody mess, my boot and trouser leg were covered in blood. I wiped off what I could with handfuls of straw, but it still looked a mess. Our new platoon commander thought I'd been shot in the leg when he saw it! I thought I shall smell very nicely in a few days time. After dark I was on guard, all the fires had burnt themselves out, but visibility still wasn't very good, when I heard something coming up the road. It was a muffled sound but I couldn't identify it, so I woke Tom. We turned the Bren gun round and waited. Out of the mist and smoke loomed a tall figure in a beret.

'Halt!' I called out.

The figure stopped and called out his rank and name, 'First Commando Brigade.'

The column slowly continued up the road towards the river Aller. I then realised why I hadn't recognised the sound, Commandos boots had got thick rubber soles, not the standard issue leather and studs like us. We wished them good luck and settled down again; very glad we hadn't got the job they'd got to do tonight! During the night they crossed the river Aller, mainly using the railway bridge a little further downstream and established a small bridgehead between there and the village of Hademstorf. They then advanced south–eastwards in order to take the road bridge from the rear. In our sector the Germans hadn't attempted to hold the far bank of the Leine in any great strength, about the Aller they were more sensitive. Strong opposition met the Commandos, the banks of the river were thickly wooded and stubbornly defended, still the Commandos pressed on. They were still two-hundred yards from the bridge when at it was blown at 2 AM. The south–west end of the span collapsed into the water, leaving a gap of 120 feet. During the next day the Commandos secured the site and held a perimeter of about 1,200 yards around it against heavy counter-attacks mounted by German marines with some tanks and armoured cars. All their efforts were repelled with severe losses, and during the evening 4th KSLI were put over the river to reinforce the brigade, while upstream at Engehausen 1st Cheshire also crossed and established a bridgehead of their own.

Now with the appearance of enemy tanks the engineers set about the problem of getting the necessary tanks and guns over the Aller. The first step was to build rafts, for until the bridgehead could be further secured, to start bridging operations would have been to court a repetition of our unpleasant experiences on the Wesser. So rafts were constructed and a squadron of 3rd Royal Tanks were ferried across to support the Commandos. On the other flank the Cheshires moved westwards from their bridgehead and finally linked up with the Commandos. But our attention was somewhat distracted from these movements by an event of quite a different nature. For it was at this stage that we first heard the name of Belsen.

We thought we were held up because of the blown bridge, but this was not strictly the case. The German garrison commander suddenly appeared under a flag of truce and requested a meeting with our Corps Commander. He was anxious that the area around the camp at Belsen should not become a battlefield and the possible escape of some of the camps sixty-thousand prisoners because of the possible spread of typhus, one of the camps more repellent features. In exchange he would give us free passage, including the bridge over the Aller at Winsen. The restriction zone proposals were so arranged as to be tactically unfavourable to us and were rejected. Instead a local agreement was concluded fixing a limited typhus zone around the camp itself. The enemy there upon blew the Winsen Bridge, but by the morning of 13th April we had one of our own at Essel, just a few miles from our present position. We didn't waste any time and by mid-morning we were crossing the Aller over the new bridge. It was a sad sight to see lined up along the grass verge the fatal casualties from the assault on the bridge, especially after all their efforts to capture the bridge intact had ended in failure. We hadn't a clue where we were going today, except we were following the river upstream, so we just assumed we were getting back onto our original line of advance.

It was a lovely stretch of countryside; this whole area was covered by woodland, mainly silver birch, with the trees coming right up to the roadside in many places. Just about the worst possible conditions for an armoured division to operate in. Two men and a boy could hold up the whole column for hours with just a few bazookas and a machine gun! When we reached the perimeter held by 1st Commandos brigade it was now our turn to fan out and systematically clear the woods we'd been allotted. Meanwhile 1st Cheshires continued eastwards heading for the town of Winsen, supported by the 15/19th Hussars who had joined them, they pressed on resolutely along the road itself. Resistance was tough, and the Cheshires fought admirably to overcome enemy positions in the roadside woods. During the day they destroyed eleven anti-tank guns and took over two-hundred prisoners. We had a comparatively easy day compared with the Cheshires, and by evening had reached the Winsen-Ostenholz road, thus cutting off any escape in that direction for the Winsen defenders.

Stiff opposition continued however, and the following day at 1200 hours the Cheshires were still two miles short of Winsen. We were in a favourable position sitting to the northwest of the town and were asked to assist the Cheshires and launch an attack from that direction. The battalion lined up in the woods on either side of the road and when the tanks from the 2nd Fife and Forfar Yeomanry arrived our advance on the Winsen defences began. As we slowly moved through the trees we could hear the shells from our 25-pounders exploding in front of us, some I thought a bit close! For the next thirty minutes we picked our way through the trees, our main problem was keeping our lines straight as we advanced through the more dense parts of the wood. With our own artillery shelling in front of us this was important as you can well imagine. We were lucky because we were next to the roadway; we just kept level with the leading tank. We didn't see any sign of the enemy in the woods at all, and in front of us we were approaching the last of the trees, beyond them were open fields. About half a mile away we could see the town of Winsen, the houses and church spire were visible above the trees. Before we broke cover and moved into open country we stopped and waited for everyone to catch up. I was only about ten yards from the road, and from my position, through a gap in the trees, I could see right down the road. I noticed some movement on the grass verge about 200 yards away, no doubt in my mind it was a German soldier. I called out to Jim our section leader, who came across in front of me, and like me got up on one knee to get a clearer view through the trees and undergrowth. I never had the time to answer his question, one second later he was dead. The snipers bullet hit him straight between the eyes, blew a large hole in the back of his steel helmet and ripped the epaulet off the shoulder of my battledress blouse, an inch lower and it would have smashed my collar-bone. I've never hit the ground so fast, for a second Jim didn't move, then slowly toppled over on his side, the blood pouring from the hole in his head. Behind me someone murmured 'bloody hell' and slowly repeated it over and over again. A few yards to my left: Jim's mate, a young lad, was sobbing his heart out. He started to crawl towards Jim's body and tried to grab his hand. I shouted to him to keep down, there was nothing he could do for Jim now. Mercifully while manoeuvring, the leading tank knocked down a small silver birch tree that fell right across Jim's body, hiding it from our view. The tank then opened fire on the church; it didn't take many rounds to destroy the steeple. I hadn't moved, the shock and realisation of what had happened, the thought that I was probably the snipers original target, and if I hadn't called out to Jim, he would be alive now, and I would be the one dead.

At this point, one of the section climbed onto the leading tank and informed the tank commander about the sniper and where he was hiding. What happened next surprised everyone, the tank took off down the road like a scalded cat, ran onto the grass verge, stopped with its one track over the snipers trench and spun round several times compressing the soil on top of the sniper, burying him alive. We were unaware of the events that had taken place over to our right, the survivors from 8 platoon began to appear, carrying their wounded towards the road, they'd had the misfortune to be caught by a salvo from our own 25 pounder shells and had sustained heavy causalities. A Company was having a bad day and we hadn't even reached the town yet.

The order came down the line to move out, we climbed aboard the tanks and headed down the road towards the town, passing the spot where the sniper was buried. We got as far as the first buildings before we came under small arms fire. The tanks began blasting everything in sight, and we began the task of clearing each house in turn, as slow, tedious and dangerous job. The German infantry were popping up all over the place and we had a series of running battles between the houses and gardens. With Jim gone, our section was a bit like a ship without a rudder, but we'd done it all before so we soon adapted to the new situation. It was ten o'clock in the evening before we fully occupied the town; our only source of light was from the burning buildings. The last two hours had been hectic and spectacular with the tracers from the tank machine guns flying in all directions, and the 77 mm explosive shells from their big guns scattering debris from the burning buildings high into the air, showering us with sparks, it was like the 4th July and Bonfire night rolled into one. But we always tried to leave a few houses undamaged where possible to sleep in.

The 1st Cheshire moved forward and by the next morning Winsen was completely clear. Our dead could be counted on one hand, but the Cheshires suffered heavier casualties, with fourteen dead and many more wounded. I shall never forget the events that took place on the 14th April 1945.

We also had a new section leader today, a corporal from one of our other platoons. His name was Len – a Brummie – and a completely different character to Jim. Of cause we didn't know yet what his leadership qualities were like.

29th Armoured Brigade advancing northwards from the Essel Bridge itself became more and more unpromising. It was therefore decided to abandon the effort in this area and move 29th Armoured Brigade group along behind 159th Brigade as far as Winsen, from there 29th would take the left route and 159th the right. The bridge at Essel was finally dismantled after a new bridge was built at Winsen. So both brigade groups turned north. The 23rd Hussars and 8th Rifle Brigade led off. After the town of Walle was cleared, opposition ceased. Naturally the Germans were not prepared to resist in the vicinity of Belsen. The concentration camp itself was passed in the afternoon. On the right route we took the lead with our old friends the 2nd Fife and Forfar Yeomanry. Our objective was the town of Walthausen. It wasn't an easy morning, we had to deal with roadblocks, bazookas and anti-tank guns which continued to obstruct our progress as far as Hessel. But from there onwards progress was fast. We sat on the backs of the tanks, and raced along, and by evening the leading tanks had reached Munden. By now with very little sleep last night we were all tired and hopeful of a quiet peaceful night. What happened next scuppered any chance of that! After the first squadron of tanks were over the bridge, it was blown, thus leaving them on the far side of the river in the gathering dusk without any infantry support. A Company drew the short straw and were soon over the river to support the tanks. We soon engaged the small demolition party, killing three and capturing the remainder. Our new company commander Major Tapper, a big man, was cheered by the lads as he grabbed two German soldiers by the scruff of their necks, and frog marched them down the road. Our next job was to form a bridgehead and hold it until our engineers could build a new bridge. This they did under cover of darkness. It was completed by 1030 hours the following morning. The remainder of the regiment then joined the two troops and the whole group pushed on towards the next village, a small place called Poitzen. We had no problems and reached our objective by midday. At the next village we were called to a halt, the route we had opened was assigned, almost at once to 29th Brigade Group. Their line of advance on our left had come to nothing, all the bridges in the area were blown, the tracks were of poor quality and the enemy were everywhere. A Company dug in around a small village while 29th Brigade passed through. Our platoon dug in on a piece of waste ground near the edge of a wood. On the other side of the road was the village school. We could hear the children playing while we dug our trenches. The cook's wagon set up behind the school and started to prepare our meal. When it was ready, each section went in turn. I stopped behind on the Bren gun, when our turn came. While they were away I noticed someone peering at me through the trees from the edge of the wood after a few minutes a strange figure stepped into the open, and after a moments hesitation slowly walked towards me. I couldn't believe my eyes, in front of me stood someone looking like Ben Gunn out of Treasure Island, his clothes were in tatters, he'd got hair down to his shoulders, a long beard and was absolutely filthy. In a very quiet voice he asked,

'Are you English?'

'Yes,' I replied.

He slowly started to smile, then jumped up and down waving his arms about. I looked on in disbelief. Finally he calmed down, and told me who he was. He was a British soldier taken prisoner in 1940, escaped from a prisoner of war camp and had been on the run for about two years living mainly off the land. He didn't even know D-day had taken place. Suddenly he turned round and headed back for the woods. I shouted,

'Where are you going?'

He stopped and replied, 'I'm going to get my mate, there's two of us.'

No sooner had my unexpected visitor disappeared into the trees than I heard the lads returning across the playground. I thought if I tell them what's happened they'll never believe me! I turned round in time to see Tom carrying my dinner across the road onto the waste ground, the rest of the section strung out behind him. On the edge of the playground nearest to the road was a small square toilet block containing several toilets, a woman with a small child was about to enter the first one. I noticed them because the child was crying. Tom was about ten yards away when suddenly we heard the noise of a Moaning Minnie, there was no mistaking the roar as each barrel fired, and the scream from the sirens as the bombs came towards us. I dived into the bottom of our trench as Tom came tumbling in on top of me. A few seconds later the first bomb exploded right on top of the pile of soil we'd dug out of our trench, the rest of the salvo fell right across the village. The next minute was probably the most frightening of my life, I couldn't move, I couldn't breath, I felt as if I was being crushed to death. I heard the explosion from the bomb, then complete silence as the side of the trench collapsed on top of us.

The next thing I knew, Tom was tugging on my arm trying to pull me clear. I struggled to my knees, then sat on the side of the trench gasping for breath. Looking around I was just in time to see the woman and child stagger from what was left of the toilets. It had received a direct hit and was almost completely destroyed. It was a miracle they'd escaped with only cuts and bruises. We had one casualty; Ted Bishop received shrapnel wounds from the bomb that hit the toilet. There was only on fatality from the attack. A woman was hanging out her washing, when one of the bombs fell on a nearby woodpile she was decapitated by a piece of flying timber. Once I'd recovered, my first thought turned to food. I found my mess tins eventually, full of soil and what was left of my dinner. That meant nothing to eat for me tonight; I just tightened my belt and lit a cigarette.

That night our section slept in a bungalow, taking over the one large room and slept on the floor. There was a middle aged woman and her daughter living there, and although we tried to speak to her, she never uttered a word all night. I realised later she must have been terrified of what we might do, especially with her sixteen year old daughter asleep in the next room. She sat all night on a hard chair outside the door of her daughter's bedroom, never moving once. She needn't have worried; our minds were more on survival, and whether we would still be around tomorrow night. We were up and on the move again at first light. Our original route had been taken over by 29th Armoured Brigade, so we had to find another route to their right by using the minor road from Hermannsburg. This was made possible by the capture intact of the eastward bridge out of Hermannsburg yesterday. The enemy was now employing every delaying tactic he could, each morning the leading tanks ran into roadblocks, mines or men concealed at the side of the road with bazookas. This gave his retreating troops more time to escape across the river Elbe. Our advance continued relentlessly, towns and villages were captured one after the other. On our left 7th Armoured Division were coming up at quite a pace, but our divisional commander was quite determined to be the first British troops to reach the great river. On the whole we thought we'd got an excellent chance. By the afternoon we found ourselves clearing a large village, suddenly we came under sniper fire from several houses. The response from the tanks was devastating, in minutes every house was ablaze and any sniper trying to escape the flames was quickly dealt with. The road running out of the village was typical, with an avenue of trees running along each side of the road. Our section was slowly moving up the road, when I walked straight into a wire stretched across the road. One end was fixed, the other end went round the trunk of the tree opposite and on to the trigger of a bazooka. I just had time to run in front of the leading tank and stop it just before it reached the wire. That brought the column to an halt, then everyone wanted to examine this ingenious booby-trap. Meanwhile Tom and I moved up the road to the last house, and sat on a nice grassy bank by the driveway, and had a smoke. We then walked up the short drive and went into the house through the front door, the top floor was well alight. After a quick look through the front rooms, we went down the hall into the kitchen at the rear of the house. We were looking through the cupboards when there was an almighty explosion. We both dived head first through the kitchen window, landing on the garden amongst broken glass and splintered window frame, just as the ceiling came crashing down.

'What the bloody hell was that?' Tom asked, knocking the dirt and glass splinters off his clothes.

'Are you alright?' I inquired.

His trousers were ripped just above the knee and he'd got a slight cut. I was alright not a scratch.

There were a few anxious faces awaiting us, when we made our way round to the front of the house, and when we looked back you could see why! The whole front half of the house had gone, and the roof had collapsed. Where Tom and I had been sitting was a large crater, we'd only been sitting on a concealed five-hundred-pound bomb! By now the platoon commander arrived, he examined the area around the crater and pointed out the two detonator wires running along the ditch up the road. Luckily no one else had been hurt by the explosion. That booby-trap, stopping the column like it did may have saved a few lives. We were about to continue on our way up the road, when suddenly two German soldiers jumped up out of the ditch about one hundred yards in front of us, and ran across the road into some trees. From my position there was a chance they'd pass through an opening in the trees. I took the safety catch off my rifle and got down on one knee and waited. Sure enough, one of them appeared in the gap running away from me, I managed to fire two quick shots, I saw a puff of dust as my second shot hit the middle of the pack on his back. He stumbled and fell flat on his face, he didn't move again. The second one was shot by one of our other platoons a short time later. Tom gave me a wry smile,

'Lady luck was smiling on us today Bob.'

That night we dug in on the outskirts of another small village. I'd told Tom and the rest of the section about the encounter I'd had with the escaped prisoner of war yesterday. We were all wondering whether they'd turned up this morning after we'd left. Unfortunately we were never able to find out what happened to them.

Large towns are rarely given as objectives for armoured divisions, that is not their job, unless it is anticipated that they are only lightly defended. The regiment that gave us that information was the Inns of Court, our reconnaissance regiment, I don't think I've mentioned them before because we only saw them on very rare occasions, and then it was only a fleeting glance as they raced by in their Daimler and Humber armoured cars. Theirs was a dangerous job, probing forward miles in front of everyone else, and also covering the flanks of the armoured columns. The information they sent back was vital for the division's success.

In our line of advance lay the large town of Luneburg. That was to be the division's next objective, so at 0930 hours on the morning of April 18th the advance began. If it proved difficult, the task would be handed over to the 15th Scottish Division, and the 11th Armoured would bypass the town to the west. The first troops to enter Luneburg were the Inns of Court, closely followed by 15/19th Hussars. Another squadron of Hussars with a company from the 1st Cheshires entered the town from the west. Little opposition was met it was becoming increasingly obvious the enemy were on the run, and trying to get on the other side of the river Elbe as fast as possible. The remainder turned north, and occupied the town of Bardowich. It was now our turn. We passed through them in an effort to reach Winsen. This was a much larger town than the other Winsen on the River Aller. Everything went fine until we reached the village of Rottorf about five miles short of our objective. There the bridge was blown after four of our tanks had crossed A Company went over the river to lead the attack with the support from the four stranded tanks. Rottorf was a typical German village of this region. The houses were well scattered on either side of the main road, all standing in their own plot of land. Any other roads were only dirt tracks. Each family seemed to live off this small plot of land and most of the houses had barns built on the back where they kept the cattle. In the lofts they stored last years hay to feed the cattle through the winter. Unfortunately for them this type of building, which was largely constructed of timber, was very easy to destroy with the minimum of effort on our part. The tank machine gun ammunition contained incendiary rounds; so one short burst of fire just under the eaves was all that was needed to set the building on fire. We approached the village using the tanks as cover until we got closer; the turret machine guns broke the silence, as most of the houses were systematically destroyed. Each platoon cleared a different part of the village, we went straight down the main road to the far end of the village taking one of the tanks with us, clearing houses as we went, up to now we'd only found very frightened civilians. By now it was getting dark, and as we approached the last few houses I remember how thirsty we were. The last house on the left was well alight, but on the right, a large house, we'd deliberately left intact to sleep in. Next to it was a bungalow, the occupants, an old couple were crouching in the doorway, absolutely terrified. Simo the Bren gunner put his arm round this little old lady and tried to reassure her that we weren't going to burn down their house. Then he made gestures to them that we were all thirsty. The old man soon understood what we wanted and disappeared into the house, returning with a bucket of milk, that's all they'd got. With all the smoke my tongue felt like a crisp, the milk tasted great, it didn't take us long to empty the bucket. Simo gave the old man a cigarette and persuaded them they'd be a lot safer indoors. With all our allotted houses cleared we crossed the road and settled down in a deep ditch, which ran down the left hand side of the main road. The last house on the left as I've mentioned was now burning well, the flames were coming out of all the upstairs windows sending sparks flying high into the air. It was then we noticed someone come out of the house carrying two chairs. He put them down on the grass about halfway between us and the house, then dashed back in again, this time he struggled out with a table. He couldn't see us in the ditch, the only light was from the fire. Suddenly one of the lads jumped up ran across and grabbed the two chairs and concealed them back in the ditch. Each time he brought a piece of furniture out of the burning building, two of the lads fetched it and put in out of sight. The poor chap couldn't understand where his furniture was disappearing to, but he also couldn't stop to find out, because there wasn't much time left before the ceilings would collapse. Finally he had to give up when it became impossible to beat the heat and flames; he sat on the last surviving chair, a picture of despair. The platoon sergeant broke up our little game, our section was given the job of checking one of the remote farms on the outskirts of the village, We split up on reaching the farm, some checked the outhouses, others the house. Tom and I did the cellar. The entrance was outside, down some steps, through a door into a long corridor. We couldn't see a thing, I remember finding a doorway by feeling along the wall. We pushed the door open and stepped inside. I found a match and struck it on the wall. I couldn't believe my eyes, sitting on benches along three side of the room were about twelve fully armed German soldiers and two women. Nobody made a sound. The match went out! I had to strike another match to make sure I hadn't imagined it. Sure enough there they were, sitting as quiet as mice. One of the women lit a candle giving us more light. Looking round their very young faces I quickly realised we hadn't got anything to fear. They were terrified of us, one sharp command and they put their hands on top of their heads and we marched them back down the road. We then dug in around the large house we'd left undamaged, two of the section stopped outside on guard, the rest of us went indoors.

While we'd been away the cooks had prepared a meal and brought it over to us, we were starving. The room we were in had got a single oil lamp on the table, and behind it a mirror hanging on the wall. I didn't recognise my own reflection, no wonder the Germans were frightened – it frightened me! I hadn't had a wash or shave since leaving Holland, my face was black with lighter streaks from the sweat that had run down my brow, and finally black stubble on my chin. My battledress was filthy with small rips and snags everywhere, the front of my blouse was spattered with blood and the one trouser leg was now dark brown and stiff with the blood from the dead cow. Looking around the room at one another, no wonder the three women in the room with us were shaking, from their point of view we must have looked like savages. There was middle-aged woman and her teenage daughter, and a very smartly dressed woman in her late twenties with a young baby. We found out she was an evacuee from the city of Hamburg. Before we settled down for the night Tom asked the woman for a needle and thread to sew the long rip in his trousers. When she produced her sewing basket, Tom insisted that her daughter did the sewing, much to the concern of the mother. This meant putting her hand up Tom's trousers to hold the material away from his leg. With a shaking hand she repaired the rip and made a good job of it under the circumstances, much to the relief of the mother. That little drama over we settled down for the night.

The following morning the whole company stood-to, an hour before dawn until first light. It was a very dark morning with no light from any source. All the fires had burnt themselves out, but the smell of smoke still lingered on the still air. Everyone was very quiet; we knew our position was very vulnerable. The tanks had moved back to the centre of the village with the three platoons from our company spread out around them. Around the perimeter of the village was dense woodland, an ideal place for the enemy to launch a counter attack. We quietly waited in our dugouts. Suddenly those first rays of light appeared on the horizon, slowly spreading upwards and outwards. A new day had begun. Dawn has always been a special time for me, especially in spring with dawn chorus from the birds, and those clear brilliant sunrises. Today it signified a more sinister time, the most vulnerable time for the enemy to attack. To me it meant I'd survived another night! We finally stood down and had an early breakfast. It was a misty morning and with the smoke from last nights fires, visibility was poor. Simo was on guard in the ditch at the side of the road facing towards Winsen. Suddenly he heard someone singing and footsteps coming down the road towards him. He quietly waited, finger lightly on the trigger of the Bren gun. Out of the mist marched a uniformed figure singing away as if he hadn't got a care in the world. Simo waited patiently until he was only a few yards away, then stood up and screamed,

'Halt!'

As you can imagine he nearly died of shock, his shoulder bag fell to the ground and his hands shot into the air – it was a German pilot coming home on leave. I'm afraid his leave would now be rather extended.

At about nine o'clock the enemy suddenly opened fire on our positions with mortar and machine guns from the surrounding woods. Luckily for us he didn't follow up with an infantry attack. We called on our 25-pounders who soon blasted the village perimeter. The enemy soon withdrew, while the whole incident only lasted about fifteen minutes. Unfortunately one of the tank crews, who were having their breakfasts outside their tank, suffered casualties: two were killed others wounded. By mid-morning the bridge was completed, and the remainder of the brigade began passing through us on their way to the large town of Winsen. We followed them later in the day.

The capture of a bridge over the river Elbe had not been seriously considered but at this stage anything was possible. To the east of our position the 4th KSLI and the 3rd Royal Tank Regiment had won the race to the river, arriving there on the morning of April 19th. It was then confirmed that the railway bridge at Lauenburg a few miles away was still intact. By midday the KSLI were at grips with the enemy, who were defending the embankment on our side of the river, a force of about two-hundred men and one Tiger tank. They were supported by artillery fire from the other side of the river. Our 25-pounders soon engaged the enemy artillery, knocking out several guns, and during the afternoon the KSLI closed in, taking fifty prisoners and killing about twenty of the enemy. By 1700 hours they controlled most of the area on our side of the river, 3rd Royal Tanks were only about two-hundred yards from the bridge when there was a loud explosion. The bridge was no more!

Yesterday afternoon the 23rd Hussars fought one of the strangest engagements of the war, against a circus. Briefly the report stated that three bears had been wounded, three lions escaped and two elephants captured intact. How this case of mistaken identity arose was not revealed.

We arrived in Winsen in the afternoon, and were immediately given the task of clearing a section of the town. This meant systematically going through each house, street by street. A long, tedious and time consuming job. I remember two incidents that occurred on that first day. One was life threatening, the other was of a more pleasant nature.

We were checking a row of terraced houses, Tom and I were entering each house from the rear, while Simo and his number two were coming through the front. At this one house he found the door locked, and without thinking, stepped back and blew the lock off with a burst of fire from the Bren gun. This happened just as I was about to open the back door. It was a straight-through hallway. The back door was half glazed, which shattered all around me as the rounds from the Bren whistled past my head. How I escaped not being hit I will never know. I called him a few 'choice' words; he just grinned and said,

'Sorry Bob!'

Later I found myself in a house on my own, everyone else seemed to have disappeared. In one of the bedrooms I found a woman, she was about twenty-five years old, very attractive, but looking very frightened when I pushed the door open. Before I could say anything she asked me if I was Canadian,

'No, British.' I replied.

She seemed quite relieved and put her arms around my neck and kissed my cheek, tears running down her face. She then told me what she was doing in Germany. She was an American that had been caught in Germany when the war broke out and had been unable to leave the country when the borders were closed. Her passport had been confiscated and then she had been made to work in the local hospital. I always felt that she didn't tell me the full story, but I never saw her again; although she did try to find me on a couple of occasions while we were stopping in Winsen. I discreetly kept out of her way, much to the amusement of the rest of the section.

Since leaving the river Aller we had travelled fast, sixty miles in five days. Advancing at this pace it was not possible to account for all the enemy troops in your area. Some were by-passed because they weren't on our main line of advance, others in small remote villages had no idea they'd been by-passed. Many for example employed on static installations, such as airfields, had surrendered 'en masse', but others, whose retreat had been cut off, would take to the woods and lie low until the forward troops had passed through, then attack the supply columns. Now the division had reached the Elbe this was one of the problems that had to be addressed, and speedily dealt with! Our immediate task was to clear the riverside villages between Winsen and Niedermarschacht, while preparations were made for the assault across the Elbe. By the 27th April, all the enemy forces in our region had been captured or eliminated.

This gave us a chance to pull back a few miles for a well-earned rest and recharge our batteries in preparation for the final battle.

Our billet was a large house with a nice garden. We'd all got beds to sleep on, and for the first time since leaving the battle school in Holland, I was able to undress to go to bed. Considering I hadn't had my boots off for nearly a month, my feet were pretty good – I couldn't say the same thing about my socks and underclothes. I shall not forget that first night. I slept ten hours straight off, instead of the usual two or three. No guards, no stand-to. The next day we were able to wash and shave, and get clean socks and underclothes. I also saw Maurice again for the first time since leaving the battalion in Belgium, collecting some prisoners. Prisoners were now becoming a big problem, with hundreds coming in every day.

It was thought possible that with the Russians now approaching swiftly from the east, it might induce the enemy beyond the Elbe to lay down his arms and allow us free passage. We knew that the troops on the spot were amenable to certain proposals, but to procure any agreement from their higher commanders was impossible. Even in their hour of defeat the discipline of the German forces remained such that open violation of orders was unthinkable. With the breakdown of these local negotiations, our original plan for the assault across the river went forward. The assault force would consist of the 15th Scottish infantry division, supported by the 1st Commando Brigade. After bridges had been constructed at Lauenburg and Artlenburg and the bridgehead enlarged 11th Armoured Division were to pass through the Scotsmen and continue the advance towards Lubeck and the Baltic coast. The attack was scheduled to start at 0200 hours on the morning of April 29th.

The operation had a number of phases, and when we'd make our move would depend on the success of these. We were scheduled to cross at midday on May 1st. Meanwhile, after rearming the men and materials, we rested and waited for the call to move out. We didn't have to wait too long, the work on the Artlenburg bridge was so promising that we were ordered to be prepared to cross the river at 1800 hours on April 30th, nearly a day earlier than expected. Even so the roads were so congested it was 2200 hours before our first tanks crossed the river. All I can remember was it was dark when our company went across the bridge. By 0400 hours our leading tanks, 23rd Hussars with the 8th Rifle Brigade had broken out of the bridgehead perimeter and were attacking the village of Sahms. This place was well defended by quite a number of infantry with two anti-tank guns and took most of the morning to clear and produced 100 prisoners. After that, progress became easier. By first light we had cleared the bridgehead perimeter. A small bridge at Lutau had been destroyed, so the only route available was through Gulzow as far as Schwarzenbeck. From there the 23rd Hussars and the 8th Rifle Brigade took the right hand route, heading for the villages of Borstorf and Siebenbaumen. We took a more westerly route to the left, our objectives for the day were the villages of Havekost, Mohnsen and Trittau. Almost immediately we ran into trouble, roadblocks and mines soon brought the column to a standstill. Luckily for us they didn't seem to be defended, so one by one they were cleared, but progress was slow. We were travelling through woodland on both sides of the road, which meant we had to keep a sharp lookout for bazooka parties.

One roadblock stands out in my memory, a very large tree had been felled right across the road, and down the whole length anti-tank mines had been attached, we had to get the engineers to that one! Then just to stop us getting bored, a couple of Messerschmitt Bf 109 fighter planes strafed us with cannon and machine gun fire – that woke everyone up! We dived into the trees and sheltered behind the largest tree we could find. The road was cleared eventually, and we continued on our way at last, until we came to a small timbered house on the side of the road. The whole platoon went down the short garden path to check that the house was empty; we were also looking for something to drink. Tom and I were returning up the path when the company Bren gun carrier passed the garden gate. Just at that point there was a loud explosion as the carrier went over a mine. It shot into the air and turned completely over, landing upside down. The company commander and the driver were thrown clear, but the two signallers sitting either side of the engine in the back were trapped. There was nothing we could do for them. Within a few minutes the vehicle caught fire, and a short time after that the small arms ammunition it was carrying started to explode. In battle there are many ways to die, and I've seen most, but to be slowly burnt to death must be one of the worst. I shall never forget the screams that came from under that vehicle as long as I live. Entombed as they were, it was ten minutes before their screams finally ceased, although the ammunition still continued to explode for quite a long time afterwards. We left the carrier still burning on the side of the road and continued towards our first objective, the village of Havekost. After the tragic events of this morning the mood amongst the lads was more subdued in the afternoon. We weren't expecting too much trouble in the first two villages; the main enemy force was reported to be in the village of Trittau a few miles farther north. Our company divided into two groups, our platoon with four tanks from the 3rd Royal Tank Regiment set out for Havekost, the remainder headed for the village of Mohnsen. We were travelling on the backs of the tanks along an unsurfaced road, everything went fine until we came across a small river. The leading tank stopped and the tank commander inspected the bridge. It was only about twenty feet long, but constructed entirely of wood. It looked strong enough, so the leading tank lined itself up, and slowly edged forward with instructions from the commander from the other side of the river. It was tricky, the bridge was only just wide enough for the tank. The first tank slowly crossed the bridge, no problems, quickly followed by number two and three. Our section was on the last tank. Tom and I were sitting right on the back, our legs hanging over the edge. We were almost across when the bridge collapsed beneath us. My heart missed a beat, I thought this was something that only happened in films! We were left rocking slowly backwards and forwards on the far concrete parapet,

'Nobody move,' shouted the tank commander, he need not have worried, we were too frightened to breathe. I thought if it falls back into the river Tom and I would be crushed or drowned, they'd never be able to get us out. For a full minute we just sat as still as possible, the slightest movement and the front of the tank lifted off the ground. Then the commander slowly climbed out of the turret and crawled along the gun. Immediately the front of the tank went down, then the two lads nearest the front followed the tank commander across the gun. That gave us all the chance to move forward around the turret and distribute our weight to the front. This allowed the driver to slowly move forward out of danger. Afterwards standing on the parapet looking down at the debris of the bridge in the muddy water, I realised what a lucky escape we'd had. We had a cigarette, got ourselves reorganised and continued along the track towards our first objective.

Our section took the lead, closely followed by the tanks. The other sections were behind us, one over the hedgerow to our right, the other to the left, all travelling in single file. We had been walking for about thirty minutes with no sign of the village or the enemy. Just over the hedge to our left we had been joined by a railway track, and shortly afterwards the road started to go gradually downhill. This caused an embankment to form on the left, and a bank with a hedgerow on the top to the right. Our section and the tanks were now travelling down a deep gully. The other sections began to have difficulties with the territory they were walking over so the section on the right climbed down the bank and fell in behind the tanks. Corporal Stan Buttifant, who was leading his section along the side of the embankment, was also finding it more difficult to find a path through the brambles. Finally his route was completely blocked, he couldn't even get back onto the road, so they had to climb to the top of the embankment and walk along the railway track. This was a fatal mistake. No sooner had the section got onto the track than a shell exploded amongst them. Corporal Buttifant was killed instantly, four others were wounded. The survivors were distraught.

We had had a bad morning, and with the loss of Stan's section this afternoon we were having a bad day, and we hadn't even reached our objective yet! We continued down the hill, the embankment was still on our left, the bank on our right slowly disappeared giving us a good view to the front and over to the right. There was a T-junction at the bottom of the hill where our track ran into the main road. To the left it disappeared under the railway embankment, to the right it went along the side of a wooded hillside. Halfway up this hill, which was about six-hundred yards away, was a German half-track vehicle and a small squad of soldiers laying mines. Our leading tank opened fire with it's 77 mm gun, and missed. His aim was too high; the shell went harmlessly over the top of the vehicle. He never had another chance, the half-track charged up the hill and disappeared out of sight behind trees at the side of the road. We were frustrated and annoyed that we'd let the enemy escape, missing the one chance we'd had to even the score. So by the time we had got to the main road we were in no mood for compromise. To reach the village of Havekost we had to pass through a tunnel underneath the railway embankment. We didn't know what to expect on the other side, so we climbed on the tanks and charged through the tunnel one after the other in quick succession. Once clear we opened fire at everything in sight, anything that could conceal a sniper or bazooka party, very soon the whole village was well ablaze. Outside one of the houses, right in our path, was a saloon car. We drove right over it. What it looked like afterwards I'll leave to your imagination. I'd have loved to have been there when the owner returned. When the tanks had done their job, we dismounted and went through the village from house to house. We found plenty of German equipment they'd left behind, but the defenders had vanished, leaving only a few very frightened civilians hiding in bunkers dug in the gardens. We got them all out to make sure they weren't hiding anyone – they were absolutely terrified and convinced they were going to be shot. We had found civilians hiding soldiers before, but not today.

Our job here was coming to an end, we were joined by the rest of the company with their tanks. They brought us the good news that the German half-track that had escaped us, ran straight into them on the other side of the wood, and was quickly dispatched.

Our day was not over yet.

By 1600 hours we were approaching the large village of Trittau, a place that required something of a deliberate attack, and was not cleared until the evening. Many prisoners were taken. Our column then pushed on to Gronwohld. We'd had a bad day with six dead and four wounded. Understandably everyone was getting a bit jumpy. It was like the Ten Little Indians: who was going to be missing tomorrow night? Everyone knew we were now in the last days of the war, and as you can imagine the tension was getting worse every day. The sooner it was all over now the better for everyone.

Next morning following our usual practice, 15/19th Hussars with the 4th KSLI took over the lead. They ran into the usual anti-tank mines and bazooka parties as they headed north out of Gronwohld. These were soon cleared and they quickly reached the villages of Eichede and Barkhorst. Shortly afterwards they crossed the Hamburg-Lubeck autobahn. By 1500 hours they had occupied Bad Oldesloe without opposition, and one hour later Reinfeld was also seized. We followed along the same route for a time before turning east for our first objective the village of Rethwischdorf. We met some slight resistance for a time but this soon evaporated. I remember one incident that happened while Tom and I were clearing a very large house. We'd taken Simo our Bren-gunner with us for that little extra firepower in case it was needed. We'd just entered a beautiful room on the ground floor with oak panelling and luxurious carpets on the floor, when a white telephone on a small polished table behind us started to ring. It was so unexpected it made us jump. Simo swung round with the Bren and with a burst of fire blew the telephone off the table, shattering everything in the line of fire. It was just an instinctive reaction, but certainly made a mess of the telephone and the table it was on! The lower floor cleared we climbed the marvellous oak staircase to the gallery which ran round three sides of this large hall and started checking the rooms. In one of the bedrooms we found a well-dressed woman, probably in her late thirties. We took her with us and checked the remaining rooms. One was locked, which she arrogantly refused to open. Simo cocked the gun, pushed her against the wall with the muzzle pressed under her chin. She opened the door! Hiding inside the room we found a German officer, he didn't resist capture and came quietly. The woman broke down and cried when Simo marched him down the staircase. I happened to glance out of the back window before leaving the room, the courtyard was full of German soldiers. I nearly had a fit! By the time I got outside the German officer in charge had surrendered to our Company Commander. Not a bad afternoons work, twenty guns captured and five-hundred prisoners taken – a foretaste of the thousands that were to come. It came as no surprise when at 1115 hours this morning divisional HQ received orders to capture Lubeck. Originally it had been 5th Division's objective, but the speed of our advance since crossing the Elbe had put us well in front of the other divisions on our flanks. Nevertheless, it was good news. To achieve as the fruits of a long and arduous journey the capture of Lubeck would be a fitting end, and set the seal on the divisions achievements over the last eleven months.

It was about this time that my old mate Sparky was wounded. We were clearing a small village, whose name I've long forgotten, when unfortunately he was hit in the shoulder by a ricochet from one of our own tanks. At least his war was now over.

Normally 23rd Hussars and 8th Rifle Brigade would have taken over the lead, but were held up by bad roads and difficulties encountered in bringing forward supplies. So the task fell to 2nd Fife and Forfar Yeomanry and 1st Cheshires. They disposed of some slight enemy opposition at Westerau, where a prison camp of 1,600 RAF officers was liberated. Just south of Reinfeld they joined the autobahn. Meanwhile 23rd Hussars and 8th Rifle Brigade had succeeded in extricating themselves and were catching up fast. Both groups were now directed on Lubeck. At 1530 hours the 2nd Fife and Forfar Yeomanry and the 1st Cheshires entered the city. They met a little sporadic fire; otherwise the place was very quiet. The other group was now moving well, and having left the northern outskirts of Lubeck behind them were pressing on northwards towards Neustadt. In Lubeck it self, all the bridges were intact and the docks appeared to be in good working order. Soon the prisoners began coming in. This was to become a big problem over the next few days.

We didn't take any part in the capture of Lubeck, but riding on tanks of the 3rd Royal Tank Regiment we pushed northward, west of Lubeck, and accepted the surrender of Bad Segeberg, a large town on the Lubeck-Neumunster highway. We were ordered to secure the town and stay put. A Company occupied the northern end of the town on either side of the main road. Our platoon took over a large three-storied house, with company HQ in a house on the other side of the road. Our section slept in the large front room on the ground floor, the first night was a bit crowded with one of the tank crews sleeping in the same room, although they were up and gone before daylight. It wasn't until we got up that I found my rifle and boots gone. There were rifles and boots all over the place, but not mine. It took some time to sort things out, but when all the section got dressed and claimed their own rifles, I realised what had happened! In the dark, one of the tank crew had taken my rifle and boots in mistake, and left me his. The boots were my size, so that didn't matter too much, but the rifle was red rusty, where it had been lying for months on the back of a tank. It took me quite a while before I'd got it in working order again; the barrel was in a shocking state!

Today was to become one of the most memorable days of my life. On the 3rd May 1945 the war in Europe ended for us. Yesterday we were being shot at, today it was all over. It was just unbelievable. I'm afraid we went a little mad for a time. Someone found a pony and trap, and we took it in turns having rides up and down the road. We were like kids having donkey rides at the seaside. The sergeant major tolerated our mad hour, but it soon became obvious we'd got work to do.

Down the road from the north German soldiers began to arrive – some walking, some on bicycles, in fact every form of transport you could think of. Next to company HQ on the other side of the road to our billet, was a very large field, we began shepherding them into this field. There we lined them up, searched them, then moved them to the other end of the field, ready to be moved on to the prisoner of war camps. This went on all day. I never thought I should live to see the day whole German divisions surrendering to us this way. That evening ten of us marched ten-thousand German soldiers about twelve miles to the nearest stockade. I remember walking along at the head of my thousand strong column having a discussion with a German officer about the war and it's consequences. He also asked me if it was true that Hitler was dead. We'd heard this morning, so I was able to confirm that it was true. On reaching our destination we handed our prisoners over and got a lift back to Bad Segeberg. We were tired after a rather hectic but memorable day.

Arriving back at our billet, all tiredness soon evaporated when the platoon sergeant gave me the news that my name was fifth on the leave list for May. This was really the icing on the cake for me. With the war over it wouldn't be so bad to come back after my leave now. Many of my mates returning from leave over the last few months had been killed, terrible for their families who were waiting for that first letter, and receiving a telegram instead.

That night I went to sleep a very happy man. The next two days prisoners continued to arrive by the thousand, by evening on the 5th May we had taken 54,000; an estimate for the division of 70,000 would not be over-liberal, and among these were some twenty-five generals and admirals. Also today the official announcement was made that Field-Marshal Montgomery had accepted the unconditional surrender of all German forces facing 21st Army Group. Though the news of the total surrender to the allies did not follow until two days later. In the Forst Segeberg, west of our positions, a number of SS troops had decided to continue the war on their own. The German 8th Parachute Division, the enemy formation in the area, was ordered to operate against them. In due course, the SS yielded. There wasn't much love lost between the Paras and the SS.

Over the next three days German soldiers were still arriving, although in much smaller numbers. The 8th May 1945 officially became VE day. That evening, after a lovely sunny day, the whole platoon sat in the back garden of our house eating our meal together. Looking around at this happy group, I suddenly realised that I was the only one left out of the original platoon I'd joined in Normandy. I tried to remember all those missing faces, but found it very difficult. I must confess to shedding a tear and feeling a little sad. Not for long though, my sailing date had been fixed for the 15th May, just seven days from today. It was difficult to contain my excitement. Later that evening I wrote a letter to Margaret with the good news. I've just read that letter again, nearly fifty-four years after I wrote it: in it I describe the lovely garden where I'm sitting writing the letter, the neat rows of peas, shallots and spinach, the apple trees just starting to blossom, and finally I close the letter describing the beautiful red sunset, ending another memorable day.

The following day we heard that a German armoured unit wanted to surrender, but would only surrender to the 3rd Royal Tank Regiment. So we waited, rather intrigued, while negotiations took place. Apparently they'd fought against the 3rd Royal Tanks in the desert. Eventually a small convoy of trucks and halftracks arrived, and assembled in our field. What surprised us was they were still fully armed, and formed up in a defensive circle like an old western wagon train.

Negotiations continued throughout the day, but nothing was resolved before nightfall. That meant we had to put a guard on the field throughout the night. I think I must have been the first British soldier to do a guard with a fully armed German soldier – what a bizarre situation, nevertheless we got along fine. I found out his main interest was popular music and the American big bands. We ended up walking up and down the road, singing all the latest songs, much to the concern of the platoon sergeant.

The next morning the guards stood down, while the German officer in charge went off to meet our divisional commander. While he was away, the German company fell-in on the road and was inspected by one of their officers. They looked very smart in their polished jackboots and black uniforms. Whatever we thought of them they appeared a well-disciplined company, although it was obvious they were putting on a bit of a show for our benefit.

By now, as you can well imagine, we were all wondering why this unit was so special. Finally everything was resolved the next day when a team of our engineers and intelligence officers arrived and all vehicles and personnel were taken away. Apparently this German company had got a secret night vision sight fitted to their guns enabling them to fire at targets with great accuracy at night. Everyone uses night vision systems now of cause, but in 1945 we were only just developing them in this country, so this was quite a valuable capture for us. I think the Germans' main concern was that the night sight didn't fall into the hands of the Russians.

Time seemed to stand still for me over the next few days, I've never known the days drag so much, but inevitably my departure date arrived, and around ten o'clock on the Sunday morning of 13th May the transport arrived to pick me up for the long awaited journey home. I said goodbye to Tom and the lads, and after picking others up at battalion HQ we were on our way. The roads were very bad and progress slow, with many detours. Standing up in an open three-ton truck wasn't the most comfortable way to travel. Our first night we slept in a barn, the next two nights we were stuck in barracks near Osnabruck, because gales in the channel had halted all sailings. This was frustrating, but there wasn't anything we could do about it so we just had to be patient. It took two more days to reach Calais, travelling through Belgium and France by train, which was nearly as slow as by road.

I arrived in Dover early in the morning of Friday the 18th May, from then on progress became much quicker. Even so I didn't reach home until just before midnight. I didn't have to walk from Birmingham, like last time, but was dropped off at the bottom of our street by private car. This was a service run by volunteers to get servicemen home from New Street station after the public services had closed down for the day. My thoughts turned to the last time I walked up this street, that July morning ten months ago. A naive young soldier, about to go into action for the first time. Now the anguish of battle was over and the physical and mental scars would hopefully diminish with time. The moment I'd been waiting for, and at times the moment I thought I'd never see, had arrived. To describe my feelings as I opened the door would be impossible. My welcome home was overwhelming, the relief in my mother's eyes, Margaret's smile, Dad's outstretched hand, moments I shall never forget. We had got such a lot to say, we talked for hours. It was nice to finally curl up in my own bed again and have a long lie in the following morning. By the end of that first day, dressed in civvies, it was like I'd never been away. Mom and dad hadn't changed at all, Margaret was still the same lovely girl I'd said goodbye to at New Street station. It would be impossible to describe that ten days leave, it was a magical time. Even now, after all these years, reading Margaret's diary still brings a lump to my throat. We went for long walks, and one day I remember going to Malvern on our tandem. We also visited all our local beauty spots. It didn't really matter very much where we were as long as we were together. Even the weather, which was unsettled, didn't bother us very much. We didn't waste a minute, and towards the end of my leave we had a family party. But eventually the day came when I had to return to Germany. Margaret and Mom came with me to Birmingham, Dad had to go to work. Parting wasn't any easier, it never was, the only consolation that the fighting was now over. We said our goodbyes and I started my long journey back to the battalion. I felt terrible.

We arrived in Dover just after midnight; trucks then took us to my old barracks, the Duke of York's Military School high upon the cliffs. Believe it or not, but I slept in the same hut as I did on my last night with the Worcester's last July. We sailed the next morning for Calais, then at 9:30 PM that evening caught the train to Holland and finally the two-day journey across Germany. The battalion had left Bad Segeberg and moved farther north, near the Danish border, and were now in barracks on a hill overlooking the town of Flensburg. It was late on Saturday night when I arrived back, tired after my six day journey. I was very glad to see Tom again; he'd arranged a bed for me with the rest of the platoon. We talked and exchanged news. Maurice was back, but had just gone on leave. Tom was going in a week's time. The next morning, being Sunday, Tom showed me around. Arriving in the dark last night, I hadn't realised how large the barracks were. It had got it's own canteen, cinema, and every sporting facility. After a few days I settled down to this new post-war army routine, it was completely different to what I'd been used to before!

We had to attain a much higher personal standard in dress and equipment, brasses were now polished and after a week you could shave in my toecaps. I had a stroke of luck, the chance to go on a course in the battalion armourer's workshop. One man from each rifle company, that was four of us, went on this course. The idea was to have one man in each company trained to repair and maintain the company's weapons. I was in my element!

A few weeks went by. Tom and Maurice had returned from leave, and Stan returned fully recovered from his shrapnel wounds with others from our company. It had been a long time since the four of us had last been together. We went out and celebrated that night – it was like old times again. We also remembered those that were no longer with us, we were the lucky ones. Our comradeship born in battle would last for ever.

The last operation of the 11th Armoured Division in Europe was performed on 23rd May 1945. The Flensburg Government had served its interim purpose: the Grand Admiral and his associates, together with the accompanying members of the High Command of the Wehrmacht were now to be led into captivity. 159th Brigade had been in Flensburg since our entry into the district and had been forced to negotiate with the puppet administration until the arrival of General Rook's mission from SHAEF (Supreme Headquarters Allied Expeditionary Force) and this brigade was now given the task of carrying out the arrests. Accordingly, while squadrons of 15/19th Hussars moved up to cover the exits, 1st Cheshire and 1st Herefords closed in on their objectives: the massive Schloss Glucksburg on its lake, the barracks and buildings which housed the great ones of the German Army. The operation began at 1000 hours and was soon completed. Donitz, Jodl, Speer; practically all the captives came quietly. Only von Friedeburg crushed his phial of cyanide before he could be restrained. Thus did the last organised leaders of the Third Reich pass into our hands. It would be impossible to explain the achievements of the supporting services of the 11th Armoured Division, except at great length. However the following fact and figures may be of interest to readers and give them some idea of what was involved.

THE DIVISIONAL RASC (ROYAL ARMY SERVICE CORPS)

From D-day to VE-day the divisional RASC carried and issued:

  5,000,000 rations
 11,000,000 rounds of rifle and machine gun ammunition
   80,682 rounds of mortar ammunition
   50,764 rounds of tank ammunition
   580,720 rounds of artillery ammunition (25-pounder)
   17,000 rounds of AA ammunition
  6,000,000 gallons of petrol

It took 1000 gallons of petrol to move the division one mile.

THE DIVISIONAL RAOC (ROYAL ARMY ORDNANCE CORPS)

During the campaign the divisional ordnance services issued the following number of vehicles and stores to replace those destroyed by enemy action, or damaged beyond repair as a result of accidents.

  327 motorcycles
  140 jeeps
   74 half-tracks
  135 three-ton lorries
  198 carriers
  124 scout cars
  488 Bren guns
  476 pistols
  179 PIATs
  143 2-inch mortars
 1,166 binoculars
 2,200 watches

It is of interest that the Ayrshire Yeomanry (151st Field Regiment RA) who were in action continuously throughout the whole campaign, except for 21 days, ended the campaign with 22 out of their original 24 guns.

THE REME (ROYAL ELECTRICAL MECHANICAL ENGINEERS)

During the campaign 29th Armoured Brigade Workshops, and 159th Infantry Brigade workshops repaired between them:

    717 tanks
     40 self-propelled guns
    130 armoured and scout cars
    226 carriers
  1226 wheeled vehicles
    265 motorcycles
    233 guns of all types

TANKS

A total of 280 new tanks of all types were issued to replace battle casualties. This, together with an initial issue of 208 Comets before the Rhine crossing, means that on an average each armoured regiment had its tanks replaced two and a half times during the campaign.

PERSONAL

My own personal replacements for the campaign were:

    3 complete uniforms
    3 pairs of boots
    2 steel helmets
    4 rifles

My first rifle had the butt shattered by a shell, the second by a snipers bullet hitting the bolt, just as I was about to fire. It saved my life, but rendered the rifle useless. I lost the third in Holland when I was wounded, and the fourth was stolen on the last day of the war.

EPILOGUE

I SPENT MY last night in the army in barracks at York, sailing from Cuxhaven in Germany on the 28th June 1947 and arriving at Hull the following day. Then by train to the demob centre at York. On Monday morning the 30th June 1947, we were taken to a large hall to collect our civilian clothes. It was a bit chaotic, with everyone wandering around with armfuls of clothes, shoes and hats. I remember the smiling faces, the jokes and laughter, the almost carnival atmosphere. I chose a blue pinstriped suit, a cream shirt with maroon tie, a pair of brown shoes, and a trilby hat.

Why I picked a trilby, I'll never know. I never wore it!

I packed everything in my kitbag and with my travel documents safely in my pocket, I started the last part of my journey home. Finally after a long day, I stepped off the bus at 7:45 PM and turned into our street. I could see Margaret waiting for me by the garden gate. To describe how I felt at that moment would be impossible. Of the other reunions we'd had over the last two years since the war ended, this was the one we'd been waiting for. No more partings, no more letters to write. This was the start of a new life. Little did I know at the time how tough it was going to be.

I'd got ninety days leave and I was determined to enjoy every minute of it. I was twenty-two years old and after just completing four weeks intensive training on the Baltic coast, I knew I would never be any fitter than I was at that moment.

My problems started when my leave was over. In the last two years over one million service men had returned home, consequently there were no jobs left, no houses to live in, and the last straw no cigarettes in the shops!

Finally my uncle, Jim Gauden, who was the welfare officer at Weldall and Assembly in Old Wharf Road, Stourbridge, found me a job there. As the name implies, it was a factory producing welded fabrications. I found myself in a workshop with no windows and few electric lights. The continual noise and the smoke and fumes from the welding with no ventilation was terrible. Of course it wouldn't be allowed today, but in 1947 it was a different story. By law, working conditions improved out of all recognition in later years. After living virtually outdoors for nearly five years, you can see why I found adjusting to factory life very difficult. The work was hard, dirty, and mainly repetitious with long hours, and all for the sum of £4.70 a week! I just had to stick it out, at that time there was very little other work about. What I really missed more than anything was the comradeship. The army was like a big family. You looked out for one another, covered each others backs. Now I soon found out that in Civvy Street it was the complete opposite. The competition for work was fierce. You had to learn quickly to look after number one, or fall by the wayside. A lot of ex-servicemen were so disillusioned with civilian life they re-enlisted.

My two old school classmates I met in Normandy, Harold and Dennis Knowles from Wollescote both survived. I met Harold after the war. Unfortunately Sergeant F Tomkins from Cemetery Road, Lye, the street where I was born, died in the battle for Zomeren in Holland on the 21st September 1944. The other local lad, Private E Bedford from Brook Crescent, Wollescote was killed by a mortar bomb the following day, just a few yards from my dugout.

We were trained for battle, but it was impossible to prepare us for the mental stress of continual conflict. We had to overcome this individually. Some coped with it well, others had a bad time and it would haunt them for the rest of their lives. How can you take the life of another human being without it having some profound effect on you later in life? One lad in our company suddenly said he'd had enough, and promptly shot himself. Luckily he survived! It was a good many years before I could even talk about it to anyone. But now, after all these years, there's finally a sense of relief that I've told my story at last. I should like to thank my daughter Susan for the help and encouragement she's given me on this project, and I hope my two grandsons Jordan and Lewis will never have to experience what I went through in those historical ten months of my life.

On the 17th January 1998, Margaret and I celebrated our Golden wedding anniversary.

No better ending can be offered for this story than the words written in 1954 by Major Joe How, MC of the 3rd Battalion Monmouthshire Regiment:

'It cannot be said that these memories are happy ones, for the immediate presence of the stark tragedy of war hung as a black shroud over the period; but they are memories of a true, deep comradeship, which can only be experienced by those who live under the dark shadow of danger. They are memories of perils braved in the company of others, and friendships which, quickly matured under the common risks endured, grew in a few weeks and even days to a depth and intensity of sincerity which is incomprehensible to the uninitiated. In a world where man seems intent on destroying himself and all that he has created, in a world of violence, death and agony, where man's finer feelings are submerged in the turmoil of modern battle, the one flower which pushes its way up through the welter of debris to bloom radiantly above the orgy of destruction is the devotion of the soldier to his comrades.'

EPHEMERA

THE FOLLOWING PAGES contain a few photographs, drawings, reproductions of historical documents and a little about the author, followed by the 1st Battalion, Herefordshire Regiment Roll of Honour.

Maurice Porter, Stanley Gamble, Bob Price and Tommy Twells.

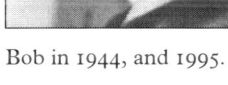

Bob in 1944, and 1995.

143

LETTER No. 3

BY THE

COMMANDER-IN-CHIEF

ON

NON-FRATERNISATION

TO ALL MEMBERS OF THE BRITISH FORCES IN GERMANY

Great progress has been made in the de-Nazification of the British Zone and in removing Nazis from all responsibility in German life. Further, the Germans have shown themselves willing to obey my orders and to co-operate in the reconstruction of their country on non-Nazi lines.

I have already modified my orders about non-fraternisation and allowed you to speak and play with little children. I now consider it desirable and timely to permit a further modification of these rules. You may now engage in conversation with adult Germans in the streets and in public places.

You will not for the present enter the homes and houses of the Germans nor permit them to enter any of the premises you are using except for duty or work.

I know the non-fraternisation policy has been a strain upon many of you who have to live and work in close contact with Germans, and I appreciate the loyal way in which you have honoured it.

B. L. Montgomery
Field Marshal,
Commander-in-Chief,
British Zone.

14 July 45.

Letter No3; announcing a relaxing of the non-fraternisation policy for soldiers in occupied Germany.

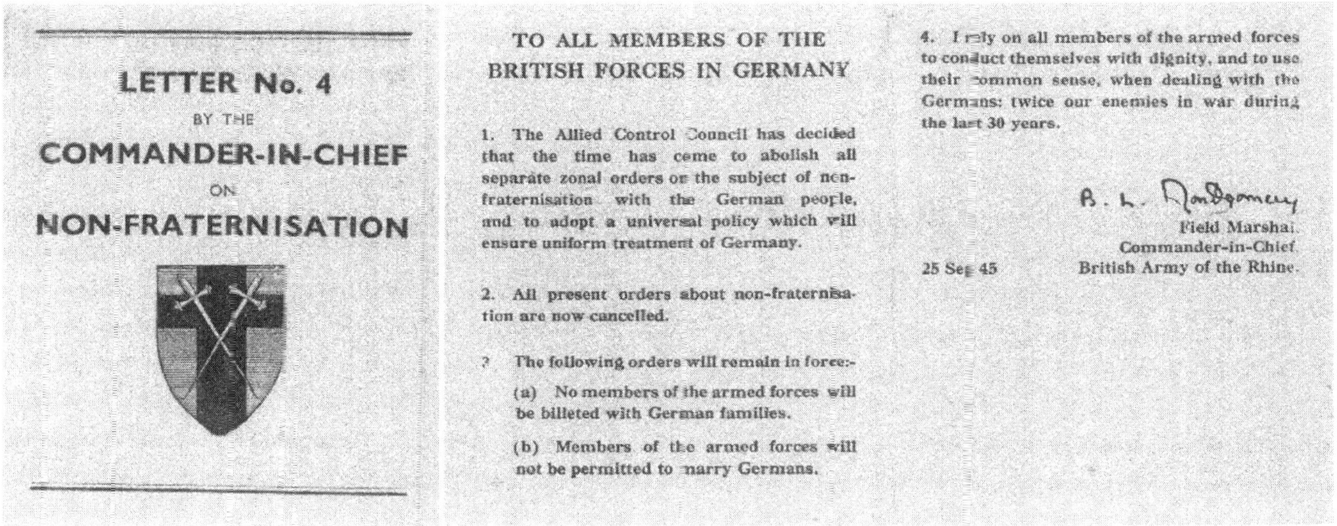

LETTER No. 4
BY THE
COMMANDER-IN-CHIEF
ON
NON-FRATERNISATION

TO ALL MEMBERS OF THE BRITISH FORCES IN GERMANY

1. The Allied Control Council has decided that the time has come to abolish all separate zonal orders on the subject of non-fraternisation with the German people, and to adopt a universal policy which will ensure uniform treatment of Germany.

2. All present orders about non-fraternisation are now cancelled.

3. The following orders will remain in force:—
   (a) No members of the armed forces will be billeted with German families.
   (b) Members of the armed forces will not be permitted to marry Germans.

4. I rely on all members of the armed forces to conduct themselves with dignity, and to use their common sense, when dealing with the Germans; twice our enemies in war during the last 30 years.

B. L. Montgomery
Field Marshal
Commander-in-Chief
British Army of the Rhine

25 Sep 45

Letter No 4, announcing a further relaxation of the non-fraternisation policy for soldiers in occupied Germany.

M4 Sherman

A34 Comet

ROLL OF HONOUR

1ST BATTALION, HEREFORDSHIRE REGIMENT

WHY IS THE roll not arranged alphabetically? By arranging the roll of honour in chronological order, I hope that what is displyed here will serve as more than just a list of names. Friends and comrades who fell together are likely to be named alongside each other and the story of the regiment's travels through Europe can be told. You can locate the towns and villages listed using the maps at the beginning and end of this book.

If you are looking for a specific name, this list also appears on my website (http://www.justawalk.co.uk/honour/) where it can be searched.

NAME	DATE	PLACE
Pte F. Ward	28/06/1944	Tourmaville
Pte V. J. Davies	29/06/1944	Tourmaville
L/Cpl W. A. Rycroft	30/06/1944	Tourmaville
Pte E. R. Higgins	30/06/1944	Tourmaville
Pte G. H. Cooke	30/06/1944	Tourmaville
Capt R. P. Barnaby	01/07/1944	Tourmaville
Cpl J. Curtis	01/07/1944	Tourmaville
Pte A. Jones	01/07/1944	Tourmaville
Pte C. Bell	01/07/1944	Tourmaville
Pte G. Lloyd	01/07/1944	Tourmaville
Pte J. Jones	01/07/1944	Tourmaville
Pte S. Evans	01/07/1944	Tourmaville

NAME	DATE	PLACE
L/Cpl A. Evans	18/07/1944	Ranville
L/Cpl D. Baker	18/07/1944	Ranville
L/Cpl R. Carey	18/07/1944	Ranville
L/Cpl T. Millington	18/07/1944	Ranville
Pte E. Andrews	18/07/1944	Ranville
Pte G. Chivers	18/07/1944	Ranville
Pte J Morrisey	18/07/1944	Ranville
Pte W. Jones	18/07/1944	Ranville
Pte A. Jones	19/07/1944	Demouville
Pte B. Ritterband	19/07/1944	Demouville
Pte B. Skinner	19/07/1944	Demouville
Pte D. Finney	19/07/1944	Demouville
Pte W. Carberry	21/07/1944	Caen
Capt S. H. Boddy	30/07/1944	Tourmaville
L/Sjt F. Jones	30/07/1944	La Vacquerie
L/Sjt T. Preedy	30/07/1944	La Vacquerie
Pte D. Deleury	30/07/1944	La Vacquerie
Pte E. Sage	30/07/1944	La Vacquerie
Pte E. Wagg	30/07/1944	La Vacquerie
Pte G. Chapman	30/07/1944	La Vacquerie
Pte G. Lenney	30/07/1944	La Vacquerie
Pte G. Meadows	30/07/1944	La Vacquerie
Pte H. Owen	30/07/1944	La Vacquerie
Pte H. Taylor	30/07/1944	La Vacquerie
Pte I. Bowen	30/07/1944	La Vacquerie
Pte J. Ford	30/07/1944	La Vacquerie
Pte J. Hill	30/07/1944	La Vacquerie
Pte J. Pouncett	30/07/1944	La Vacquerie
Pte J. Snowzell	30/07/1944	La Vacquerie
Pte L. Oliver	30/07/1944	La Vacquerie
Pte R. Ansell	30/07/1944	La Vacquerie
Pte R. Goodman	30/07/1944	La Vacquerie
Pte S. Hancock	30/07/1944	La Vacquerie
Pte S. Phillips	30/07/1944	La Vacquerie

NAME	DATE	PLACE
Pte W. Dodd	30/07/1944	La Vacquerie
Sjt R. Millward	30/07/1944	La Vacquerie
Cpl J. Harding	31/07/1944	La Vacquerie
Pte B. Poole	31/07/1944	La Vacquerie
Pte S. Cartwright	31/07/1944	La Vacquerie
Pte J. Amphlett	04/08/1944	La Biste
Pte. F Ankers	05/08/1944	La Biste
Pte W. Finnikin	06/08/1944	La Biste
Cpl H. Williams	09/08/1944	Presles
Pte A. Sharpin	09/08/1944	Presles
Pte G. Farmer	11/08/1944	Le Bas Perrier
Cpl A. Doughton	15/08/1944	Le Thiel
L/Cpl A. Hands	15/08/1944	Le Thiel
L/Cpl G. Husbands	15/08/1944	Le Thiel
L/Cpl L. Worton	15/08/1944	Le Thiel
Pte B. Pope	15/08/1944	Le Thiel
Pte F. Cutting	15/08/1944	Le Thiel
Pte S. Powell	15/08/1944	Le Thiel
Pte W. Lewis	15/08/1944	Le Thiel
Pte A. Waythe	18/08/1944	Ecouche
Pte E. Davies (70)	18/08/1944	Ecouche
Pte E. Davies (82)	18/08/1944	Ecouche
Pte H. Jones	18/08/1944	Ecouche
Pte J. Plant	18/08/1944	Encouche
Pte D. Jeffs	04/09/1944	Hechtel
Pte E. Morris	07/09/1944	Antwerp
Capt O.T. Bulmer	09/09/1944	Helchteren
Cpl E. Marks	09/09/1944	Helchteren
L/Cpl J. Jones	09/09/1944	Helchteren
Lt F. Creamer	09/09/1944	Helchteren
Pte A Robinson	09/09/1944	Helchteren
Pte A. Tye	09/09/1944	Helchteren
Pte D. Howard	09/09/1944	Helchteren
Pte W. Davies	09/09/1944	Helchteren

NAME	DATE	PLACE
L/Cpl J. Langley	10/09/1944	Hechtel
L/Sjt W. Derry	10/09/1944	Hechtel
Lt W. Kotchapaw	10/09/1944	Hechtel
Pte A. Tranter	10/09/1944	Hechtel
Pte B Stevens	10/09/1944	Hechtel
Pte F. Hemberey	10/09/1944	Hechtel
Pte S. Blount	10/09/1944	Hechtel
Pte W. Cattell	10/09/1944	Helchteren
Sjt G. Hunt	10/09/1944	Hechtel
Cpl W. Lloyd	20/09/1944	Leende
Pte F. Jones	20/09/1944	Leende
Cpl A. Burgess	21/09/1944	Zomeren
Cpl H. Lucas	21/09/1944	Zomeren
Cpt T. Nicks	21/09/1944	Zomeren
L/Cpl W. Holland	21/09/1944	Zomeren
Pte E. Fowkes	21/09/1944	Zomeren
Pte F. Littler	21/09/1944	Zomeren
Pte G. Bickerton	21/09/1944	Zomeren
Pte H. Moses	21/09/1944	Zomeren
Pte J. Wisedale	21/09/1944	Zomeren
Pte M. Gray	21/09/1944	Zomeren
Pte W. Barrows	21/09/1944	Zomeren
Pte W. John	21/09/1944	Zomeren
Pte W. Stennett	21/09/1944	Zomeren
Pte W. Summers	21/09/1944	Zomeren
Pte W. Todd	21/09/1944	Zomeren
Sjt F. Tomkins	21/09/1944	Zomeren
Cpl H. Price	22/09/1944	Asten
L/Cpl F. Smith	22/09/1944	Asten
Pte E. Bedford	22/09/1944	Asten
Pte F. Mellor	22/09/1944	Asten
Pte G. Tedstone	22/09/1944	Asten
Pte I Wycherley	22/09/1944	Asten
Pte R. Merchant	09/10/1944	Overloon

NAME	DATE	PLACE
Pte F. Gee	11/10/1944	Overloon
Pte J. Farmer	11/10/1944	Overloon
Cpl S. Lightfoot	12/10/1944	Overloon
Pte W. Jones	12/10/1944	Overloon
Pte W. Sparkes	12/10/1944	Overloon
Cpl S. Bailes	17/10/1944	Ijsselstein
Cpl T. Lord	17/10/1944	Ijsselstein
L/Cpl J Sidwell	17/10/1944	Ijsselstein
L/Sjt D. Wale	17/10/1944	Ijsselstein
Pte A. Hill	17/10/1944	Ijsselstein
Pte A. Peck	17/10/1944	Ijsselstein
Pte J. Allott	17/10/1944	Ijsselstein
Pte R. Gastree	17/10/1944	Ijsselstein
Pte R. Saunders	17/10/1944	Ijsselstein
Pte V. Donovan	17/10/1944	Ijsselstein
Sjt A. Nicholls	17/10/1944	Ijsselstein
Cpl R. Gregson	18/10/1944	Veulen
Pte E. Penn	18/10/1944	Veulen
Sjt B. Shotton	18/10/1944	Veulen
Pte D. Knight	21/10/1944	Veulen
CQMS J. French	22/10/1944	Veulen
Pte G. Price	22/10/1944	Veulen
Pte H. Phillips	27/10/1944	Veulen
Pte W. Carden	31/10/1944	Griendtsveen
Pte H. Edwards	09/12/1944	Grubbenvorst
Pte S. Loombe	25/01/1945	Heel
Cpl M. Leader	27/02/1945	Udem
L/Cpl A. Whalley	27/02/1945	Udem
L/Cpl W. Wise	27/02/1945	Udem
Pte C. Wright	27/02/1945	Udem
Pte D. Walters	27/02/1945	Udem
Pte F. Glossop	27/02/1945	Udem
Pte P. Aherne	27/02/1945	Udem
Pte W. Cooper	27/02/1945	Udem

NAME	DATE	PLACE
Pte W. Fantham	27/02/1945	Udem
Sjt W. King	27/02/1945	Udem
Pte J. Whittle	28/02/1945	Udem
Pte W. Fowles	28/02/1945	Udem
Cpl H. Wilkins	01/03/1945	Kervenheim
Cpl J Stewart	01/03/1945	Kervenheim
Pte A. Rider	01/03/1945	Kervenheim
Pte G. Palmer	01/03/1945	Kervenheim
Pte R. Holloway	01/03/1945	Kervenheim
Pte S. Chapman	01/03/1945	Kervenheim
Pte A. Hutton	02/03/1945	Kervenheim
Pte G. Bowkett	02/03/1945	Kervenheim
Pte J. Roy	02/03/1945	Kervenheim
Pte J. Sheppard	02/03/1945	Kervenheim
Pte P. Hughes	02/03/1945	Kervenheim
Pte R. Hollyman	02/03/1945	Kervenheim
Pte R. Turner	02/03/1945	Kervenheim
Cpl H. Cole	01/04/1945	Birghte
Cpl J. Young	01/04/1945	Birghte
L/Cpl J. Longdon	01/04/1945	Birghte
L/Cpl L. Redstone	01/04/1945	Birghte
L/Cpl T. Foster	01/04/1945	Birghte
Lt G. Hopkinson	01/04/1945	Birghte
Lte A. J. Spittall	01/04/1945	Birghte
Pte C. Onions	01/04/1945	Birghte
Pte D. Judd	01/04/1945	Birghte
Pte F. Carpenter	01/04/1945	Birghte
Pte G. Chapman	01/04/1945	Birghte
Pte J. Maloney	01/04/1945	Birghte
Pte K. Dowler	01/04/1945	Birghte
Pte L. Dagenhard	01/04/1945	Birghte
Pte L. Marshall	01/04/1945	Birghte
Pte R. Portch	01/04/1945	Birghte
Pte S. Mitchell	01/04/1945	Birghte

NAME	DATE	PLACE
Pte W. Smith	01/04/1945	Birghte
Pte W. Sullens	01/04/1945	Birghte
Pte. C Anstey	01/04/1945	Birghte
Sjt L. Raines, MM	01/04/1945	Birghte
CplA.Shufflebottom	06/04/1945	Schlusselburg
Pte C. Holdnall	06/04/1945	Schlusselburg
Pte J. Bushell	06/04/1945	Schlusselburg
Pte J. Haylor	08/04/1945	Mandelsloh
a/Lt T. Hancock	10/04/1945	Grindau
Pte A. Cumming	10/04/1945	Grindau
Pte C. Richardson	10/04/1945	Grindau
Pte G. Sealey	10/04/1945	Grindau
Pte R. Hewins	10/04/1945	Schwarmstedt
Pte W. Hopkins	10/04/1945	Schwarmstedt
Cpl J. Dooley	14/04/1945	Winsen
Pte C. Francis	14/04/1945	Winsen
Pte D. Pepall	14/04/1945	Winsen
L/Cpl J. McDermott	15/04/1945	Muden
Pte S. Howard	15/04/1945	Muden
Pte J. Powis	16/04/1945	Brambostel
L/Cpl P. Gurnett	17/04/1945	Eimke
Pte C. Clarke	17/04/1945	Eimke
Pte J. Bennell	17/04/1945	Eimke
Pte J. Clayden	17/04/1945	Eimke
Pte S. Jordon	17/04/1945	Eimke
Pte W. Hill	19/04/1945	Ebstorf
Pte W. Townend	19/04/1945	Ebstorf
Pte J. Enright	20/04/1945	Winsen
Pte J. Panter	21/04/1945	Winsen
Cpl S. Buttifant	01/05/1945	Havekost
Pte G. Bailess	01/05/1945	Havekost
Pte G. Bower	01/05/1945	Havekost

THANKS

IN 1946 AN officer at divisional HQ wrote a book on the 'History of the 11th Armoured Division'. In the circumstances under which the book was written, which was by the daily reports received at HQ, it is somewhat of an 'official' view. This is understandable. Nevertheless I found it very helpful, and hope I've been able to convey the other side of the story. This book also had maps so I was able to plot our movements throughout, which allowed me to paint a much broader picture of the campaign. All the facts and figures, especially the last few pages, were taken from this book. Also the 'Roll of Honour' gave me valuable information, giving as it did the rank, name, date and place where every man in the division died. A total of 1,819 men died in the division, including 215 from the Herefords. There is no record of those that were wounded but in my experience, on average in battle, for every man killed three are wounded. That means that throughout the campaign over half the division were either killed or wounded.

Also I must thank Margaret for saving all my letters, it would have been impossible to write this book in such detail without them. Reading through them again I'm surprised at the many things I'd completely forgotten all about.

I was to spend another two years in Germany before I left the army and returned home for good, two very long years. We'd won the war, now we'd got to win the peace, but that's another story!

ABOUT THE AUTHOR

ROBERT STANLEY PRICE was born on the 21st January 1925 at his father's home in Cemetery Road, Lye.

Moved to a new home in Ludgebridge Brook in 1928, known locally as 'down the spout' and educated at Valley Road Secondary Modern, Lye. Left school at Easter 1939 aged 14 years and then started work at the Co-op, Market Street, Stourbridge.

Father Stanley Price was a shoe maker and had a small cobblers shop on Lye Cross in the 1930s.

Mother Jennie, nee Gauden, came from Bromley Street, Lye. Her elder brother Councillor James Gauden was the Mayor of Stourbridge in 1953. In 1947 he was the Welfare Officer at Weldall and Assemble in Old Wharf Road, Stourbridge and was instrumental in finding me a job there after leaving the army in 1947.

The 1st Herefords route

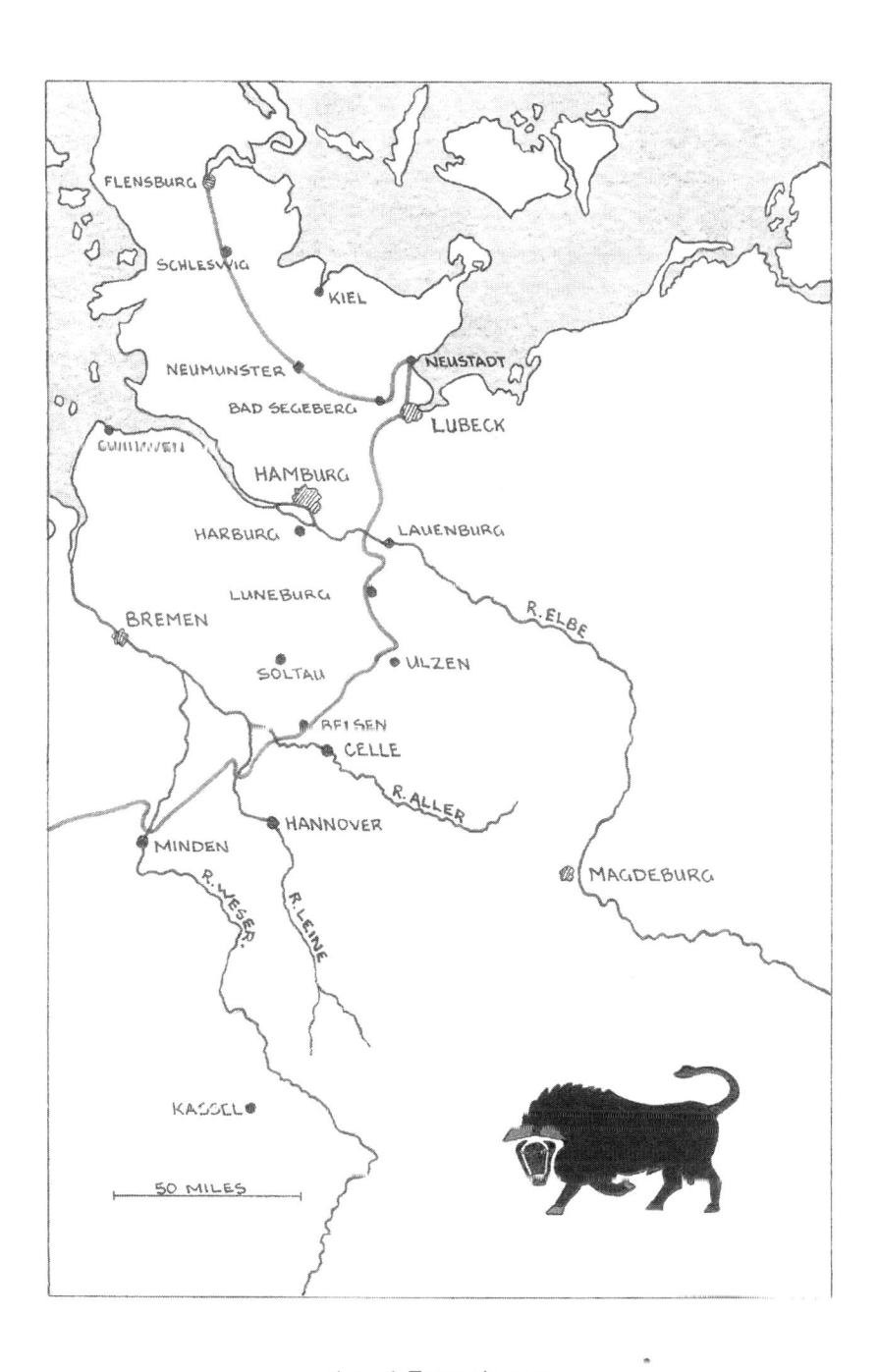

through Europe in 1945

blurb